DATE DUE

OC 7 '98			

DEMCO 38-296

Astonishing World

Astonishing World

The Selected Poems of Ángel González

1956-1986

Translated from the Spanish

by Steven Ford Brown and Gutierrez Revuelta

Edited by Steven Ford Brown

MILKWEED EDITIONS

Milkweed Editions, 430 First Avenue North, Suite 400, Minneapolis, Minnesota 55401

This edition has been translated with the assistance of the Dirección General del Libro y Bibliotecas del
Ministerio de Cultura de España.

Publication of Milkweed books is made possible by grant support from the Literature Program of the
National Endowment for the Arts, Dayton Hudson Foundation for Dayton's and Target Stores, First Bank
System Foundation, General Mills Foundation, Honeywell Foundation, Jerome Foundation, The
McKnight Foundation, Andrew W. Mellon Foundation, Minnesota State Arts Board through an appropria-
tion by the Minnesota State Legislature, Northwest Area Foundation, I. A. O'Shaughnessy Foundation,
John A. Rollwagen Fund, Star Tribune/Cowles Media Foundation, Surdna Foundation, James R. Thorpe
Foundation, Lila Wallace-Reader's Digest Literary Publishers Marketing Development Program, and by the
support of generous individuals.

Library of Congress Cataloging-in-Publication Data

González, Angel, 1925-
    Astonishing world : the selected poems of Angel González, 1956-1986 /
translated from the Spanish by Steven Ford Brown and Gutiérrez Revuelta ; edited by Steven Ford
Brown.
        p.   cm.
    English and Spanish.
    ISBN 0-915943-58-1 (alk. paper)
    1. González, Angel, 1925-   —Translations into English.
I. Brown, Steven Ford.   II. Gutiérrez Revuelta, Pedro, 1949- .
III. Title.
PQ6613.0489A22   1993   93-9273
861'.64—dc20   CIP

ACKNOWLEDGMENTS

Many of the translations in this book first appeared in the following literary journals, magazines, and newspapers: *Aura Literary Arts Review, Calapooya Collage, The Christian Science Monitor, The Colorado Review, The Connecticut Poetry Review, Gargoyle, Harvard Review, Hawaii Pacific Review, Hayden's Ferry Review, The International Quarterly, The Literary Review, The Mid-American Review, Negative Capability, Onthebus, Paintbrush, Poet Lore, Poet Magazine, Puerto del sol, Quarterly West, The Seneca Review, The Texas Review, The Webster Review, Willow Springs, The Xavier Review.*

The following journals published special features on the poetry of Ángel González: *The Connecticut Poetry Review, The Mid-American Review, Paintbrush, Poet Magazine.*

A number of poems in this book first appeared in chapbook form: *A Traveler's Notes: Five Poems,* published on the occasion of a bilingual reading of the poetry of Ángel González by Steven Ford Brown and Gutierrez Revuelta, Houston Poetry Festival (University of St. Thomas, Houston, Texas, 1987); "Before I Could Call Myself Ángel González," *The Mid-American Review Chapbook Series,* Number 12 (Bowling Green, Ohio, 1989); *Palabra sobre palabra (Word Upon Word),* published on the occasion of a reading and lecture by Ángel González, sponsored by the University of Houston, Rice University, and the Spanish Consulate (University of Houston, Texas, 1989).

"I Know What It's Like To Wait" and "So Much Universalizing" appeared in *Literary Olympians 1992,* edited by Elizabeth Bartlett (Ford-Brown & Co., Publishers, 1992).

The dialogue between Pattakos and Ritsos is from the introduction to *Fourth Dimension: Selected Poems of Yannis Ritsos,* translated by Rae Dalven. Copyright © 1976 by Rae Dalven. Reprinted courtesy of David R. Godine, Publisher.

The chronology by Paco Ignacio Taibo I is reprinted from *En homage a Ángel González: Ensayos, entrevista y poemas,* published by the Society of Spanish and Spanish-American Studies, University of Colorado, 1992).

EDITOR'S NOTE

The basis of the Spanish text used in this book is the 1986 edition of Ángel González's *Palabra sobre palabra*. Beginning in 1968, Editorial Seix Barral, Barcelona, Spain, published the collected poems of González in four editions (1968, 1972, 1977, and 1986). I consider the 1986 edition to be the definitive edition of his poems, including all changes and revisions. "The Lesson Of Literature" is not included in *Palabra sobre palabra,* so I consulted the first edition of *Grado elemental,* published by Ruedo Iberico in Paris, 1962, for the version included here. The poems in this book are ordered chronologically.

Grateful appreciation is extended to Moira Perez for her work on numerous first drafts, proofreading, and her insightful comments. Continuing support and useful criticism have also been provided by colleagues and friends: Pamela Carmell; Andrew Debicki, University of Kansas; Ana Maria Fagundo, University of California, Riverside; Fred Fornoff, University of Pittsburgh at Johnstown; Theodore Haddin, University of Alabama; David Rigsbee, Virginia Polytechnic Institute. Susana Rivera, University of Oklahoma, has contributed as a critic, facilitator, and source of encouragement. My friend Cola Franzen stepped in at the last minute to make a number of useful comments. Ángel González made suggestions on the first drafts and offered encouragement throughout the project. Grateful appreciation is extended to the Ministerio de Cultura Madrid, Spain, Frederic Ibanez Soler, Director, for financial assistance in support of this translation porject.

—Steven Ford Brown

ASTONISHING WORLD

Grado elemental (Elementary Grade), 1962

Palabra sobre palabra (Word Upon Word), 1965

Tratado de urbanismo (Treatise On Urban Development), 1967

Breves acotaciones para una biografía (Brief Marginal Notes For A Biography), 1969

Procedimientos narrativos (Narrative Procedures), 1972

Muestra, corregida y aumentada, de algunos procedimientos narrativos y de las actitudes sentimentales que habitualmente comportan (Narrative Procedures And The Emotional Attitudes That They Usually Entail), 1976

Prosemas o menos (Prosems Or Less), 1985

INTRODUCTION

Pattakos: You are a poet. Why do you get
mixed up in politics?

Ritsos: A poet is the first citizen of
his country and for this very reason it
is the duty of the poet to be concerned
about the politics of his country.

—Stelios Pattakos, vice president of
the Greek military *junta*, to Yannis
Ritsos, Greek poet, 1970

Ángel González was born in Oviedo, Spain, in 1925. His father died two
years later. During the Spanish civil war one brother was exiled and the
other assassinated. In 1944 González was diagnosed as having tuberculosis,
which led to his own exile to the mountains of León for three years.
There he began systematically to read and study poetry, especially the
poetry of Juan Ramón Jiménez and the poets of the Group of 1927 (the
poets of Lorca's generation, which includes Alberti, Aleixandre, Alonso,
Cernuda, Guillen, Prados, and Salinas). González returned to Oviedo, and
in 1949 he received his law degree from the University of Oviedo. In 1951
he moved to Madrid where his friend Carlos Bousoño, and Vicente
Aleixandre, encouraged him to publish his poems.

His first book of poems, *Aspero mundo (Harsh World)*, was nominated
for the Adonais Prize, an important literary award. Until 1972 he lived in
Madrid—with brief stays in Seville and Barcelona—and traveled to many
different European countries for short visits to participate in literary
encounters. During this period the major body of his work was published:
Harsh World (1956); *Without Hope, But With Conviction* (1961); *Elementary
Grade* (1962), winner of the Antonio Machado Prize for Poetry; *Word
Upon Word* (1965); *Treatise On Urban Development* (1967); *Brief Marginal
Notes For A Biography* (1969); and *Narrative Procedures* (1972).

In 1970 González made his first trip to Mexico and the United States
to participate in conferences and poetry readings. Beginning in 1972 he

taught at various American universities: Maryland, New Mexico, Texas, and Utah. He returned to the University of New Mexico in 1973 and has taught there since. During his American years two more books of his poetry were published: *Narrative Procedures And The Emotional Attitudes That They Usually Entail* (1976) and *Prosems Or Less* (1985).

In 1985 he was awarded the Prince of Asturias Prize, one of the most prestigious of the literary awards in Spain. In 1989 he received the Angel Maria de Lera Hispanism Award from the University of Colorado for his contributions to Hispanic culture, and in 1991 he received the International Salerno Poetry Award in Salerno, Italy.

Like the other poets of his generation, Ángel González was deeply affected by the Spanish civil war and its aftermath. He has said about that time: "I saw revolution, civil war, a dictatorship. Still in childhood, I passed in a few years from subject of a king, to citizen of a republic, to the object of a tyranny" (from the preface to an American edition of *Word Upon Word*, 1989).

His early poems, unlike the work of some of his European peers, did not revolve around the dislocated images of surrealism in a post-war world. Rather, it was his precise clarity that first brought his poetry to the attention of literary critics in Spain. Although his first book, *Harsh World*, consists primarily of short poignant nature lyrics—in both free verse and sonnet form—written in an intimate and ironic voice, the distant back-drop is the war. This book—and later books—also evidences a romanti-cism based on the transformation of nature in relation to the search for the self or a loved one. Transformations occur even in the ordinariness of every day events: spring escapes from the beak of the nightingale; the silence grows like a tree; a river changes course to follow a woman's foot-steps; a lover's body becomes a geography of hills and gardens.

This formula is repeated in his second book, *Without Hope, But With Conviction* (1961), but the vision and subject matter begin to expand and he begins to confront more directly the themes of the war. In *Elementary Grade* (1962), perhaps his finest volume, he displays the sense of con-frontation with history that characterizes his later books. In two poems on the death of Antonio Machado, "Cemetery In Colliure" and "The Lesson Of Literature," few Spanish poets have written as eloquently of Spain's defeat, or of the hope of a new Spain. It is this volume that many

Spanish literary critics point to as the beginning of his engagement with poetry as social criticism. The poems are longer and begin to take on more of a narrative structure. The poetic voice, at times, is more formal and thus less intimate, and the poet uses philosophical, religious, and scientific jargon, which serves to distance the poet from the reader. The subject matter expands to include larger issues, such as human nature, the nature (and perversion) of democracy, and the human tendency to exploit those things we come into contact with.

While the poems from *Harsh World* are almost exclusively centered in the landscapes of rural Spain, the poems of *Treatise On Urban Development* (1967) are centered exclusively in the cityscapes, often serving as metaphors for the human condition. The later poems in this volume powerfully and forcefully describe the images of war. At times one is reminded of Robert Capa's war photographs or Picasso's "Guernica." The images of war—bombed-out buildings, the rain of shattered glass after an explosion, blood on the cobblestones, abandoned automobiles, and scattered papers and photographs blowing through the streets—are made even more powerful because they are filtered through the eyes of González as a child. Because he was only eleven when the Spanish civil war began, he is able to shape experience into poems that evoke a unique innocence and poignancy. Thus the reader is allowed to move into avenues of experience that are impossible to achieve from an adult's perspective.

Many of González's poems about the civil war capture in time, like Capa's famous photographs, the indelible images of war and its aftermath that the photographer Cartier-Bresson referred to as "the decisive moment": the long lines of the defeated Spanish Loyalists marching toward the French border; the empty streets and plazas where crowds once gathered in front of the dais filled with generals making speeches; the walls of buildings where stark graffiti depicts the time of betrayal and murderers; the thunder and the wars—"the small ones that were nothing to worry about"—that frighten his mother; or the wind that blows through the deserted streets and into the fields where the wheat now grows over what was once a battlefield. If the poems of the Swedish poet Tomas Tranströmer are a meeting place, as Tranströmer himself has suggested, then the major poems of Ángel González are the place where one man confronts another against the backdrop of the Spanish civil war. He uses these images, these "decisive moments" of human conflict, to establish a moral imperative that resonates in ever-widening circles, like a stone dropped into the troubled waters of the human experience.

Brief Marginal Notes For A Biography (1969) and *Narrative Procedures* (1972) mark a shift to a kind of anti-poetry based on his belief that the written word at this point in time was useless. The subject matter touches on everything from fragments of philosophy to linguistics and word play, literary anecdote, music as public theater, science, superstition, and theater as poetry. In his last two volumes, *Narrative Procedures And The Emotional Attitudes That They Usually Entail* (1976) and *Prosems Or Less* (1985) there is a new confrontation with history: this time the history is American— North, Central, and South. His move to the United States, numerous trips to South America, and new relationships in New Mexico helped to restore his belief in the poetic word. The new landscapes and experiences also pushed him into new directions while at the same time many of the old elements and themes resurfaced: history, humor, irony, love (always distant), music, and parody.

There is a pervading sense of cynicism and solitariness in the poetry of Ángel González. It should be pointed out, however, that this pessimism has its roots in the failure of the Spanish Republic and thirty years of rule by Franco rather than in any personal failures. While it is easy to focus on these two qualities, he is ultimately a poet of connections, believing that the objects and peoples of the world are not as disparate as they seem. And, too, he has always seen himself as part of a larger group of people united by history, circumstance, and politics. Even in the poems that evidence his greatest despair, Ángel González has always understood that the poet must interpret and come to terms with the historical era in which he lives.

Steven Ford Brown
April 1993
Hyannis, Massachusetts

Astonishing
World

ÁSPERO MUNDO

1956

HARSH WORLD

1956

Te tuve
cuando eras
dulce,
acariciado mundo.
Realidad casi nube,
¡cómo te me volaste de los brazos!

Ahora te siento nuevamente.
No por tu luz, sino por tu corteza,
percibo tu inequívoca
presencia.
. . . agrios perfiles, duros meridianos,
¡áspero mundo para mis dos manos!

HARSH WORLD

I held you
when you were
soft,
cherished world.
Reality, almost cloud,
how you've flown away from my arms!

Now I feel you once again.
Not through your light, but through your skin,
I sense your unmistakable
presence.
. . . sharp profiles, hard meridians,
harsh world for my two hands!

Para que yo me llame Ángel González,
para que mi ser pese sobre el suelo,
fue necesario un ancho espacio
y un largo tiempo:
hombres de todo mar y toda tierra,
fértiles vientres de mujer, y cuerpos
y más cuerpos, fundiéndose incesantes
en otro cuerpo nuevo.
Solsticios y equinoccios alumbraron
con su cambiante luz, su vario cielo,
el viaje milenario de mi carne
trepando por los siglos y los huesos.
De su pasaje lento y doloroso
de su huida hasta el fin, sobreviviendo
naufragios, aferrándose
al último suspiro de los muertos,
yo no soy más que el resultado, el fruto,
lo que queda, podrido, entre los restos;
esto que veis aquí,
tan sólo esto:
un escombro tenaz, que se resiste
a su ruina, que lucha contra el viento,
que avanza por caminos que no llevan
a ningún sitio. El éxito
de todos los fracasos. La enloquecida
fuerza del desaliento . . .

BEFORE I COULD CALL MYSELF ÁNGEL GONZÁLEZ

Before I could call myself Ángel González,
before the earth could support the weight of my body,
a long time
and a great space were necessary:
men from all the seas and all the lands,
fertile wombs of women, and bodies
and more bodies, incessantly fusing
into another new body.
Solstices and equinoxes illuminated
with their changing lights, and variegated skies,
the millenary trip of my flesh
as it climbed over centuries and bones.
Of its slow and painful journey,
of its escape to the end, surviving
shipwrecks, anchoring itself
to the last sigh of the dead,
I am only the result, the fruit,
what's left, rotting, among the remains;
what you see here,
is just that:
tenacious trash resisting
its ruin, fighting against wind,
walking streets that go
nowhere. The success
of all failures. The insane
force of dismay . . .

Aquí, Madrid, mil novecientos
cincuenta y cuatro: un hombre solo.

Un hombre lleno de febrero,
ávido de domingos luminosos,
caminando hacia marzo paso a paso,
hacia el marzo del viento y de los rojos
horizontes—y la reciente primavera
ya en la frontera del abril lluvioso . . . —

Aquí, Madrid, entre tranvías
y reflejos, un hombre: un hombre solo.

—Más tarde vendrá mayo y luego junio,
y después julio y, al final, agosto—.

Un hombre con un año para nada
delante de su hastío para todo.

HERE, MADRID, 1954

Here, Madrid, nineteen
fifty-four: a man alone.

A man filled with February,
greedy for luminous Sundays,
making for March step by step,
towards the March of wind and red
horizons—and the recent spring
already on the edge of a rainy April . . . —

Here, Madrid, among streetcars
and reflections, a man: a man alone.

—May will come later, then June,
July after that, and, finally August—.

A man faced with a year of nothing
and his boredom with everything.

CUMPLEAÑOS

Yo lo noto: cómo me voy volviendo
menos cierto, confuso,
disolviéndome en aire
cotidiano, burdo
jirón de mí, deshilachado
y roto por los puños.

Yo comprendo: he vivido
un año más, y eso es muy duro.
¡Mover el corazón todos los días
casi cien veces por minuto!

Para vivir un año es necesario
morirse muchas veces mucho.

BIRTHDAY

I notice it: how I'm slowly getting
less certain, confused,
dissolving in the daily
air, coarse
tatter of myself, frayed
and ragged at the cuffs.

I understand: I've lived
another year, and that's a hard thing to do.
To move one's heart almost a hundred
times a minute every day!

Just to live a year one has to
die over and over.

MUERTE EN LA TARDE

De los cientos de muertes que me habitan,
ésta de hoy es la que menos sangra.
Es la muerte que viene con las tardes,
cuando las sombras pálidas se alargan,
y los contornos se derrumban,
y se perfilan las montañas.

Entonces alguien pasa pregonando
su mercancía bajo la ventana,
a la que yo me asomo para ver
las últimas farolas apagadas.

Por la ceniza de las calles cruzan
sombras sin dejar huellas, hombres que pasan,
que no vienen a mí ni en mí se quedan,
a cuestas con su alma solitaria.

La luz del día huye hacia el oeste.
El aire de la noche se adelanta,
y nos llega un temor agrio y confuso,
casi dolor, apenas esperanza.

Todo lo que me unía con la vida
deja de ser unión, se hace distancia,
se aleja más, al fin desaparece,
y muerto soy,
    . . . y nadie me levanta.

DEATH IN THE EVENING

Of the hundreds of deaths that inhabit me,
today's is the one that bleeds the least.
It's the death that comes in the afternoon,
when the pale shadows lengthen,
the contours collapse,
and the mountains are in profile.

Then someone passes by announcing
his wares beneath the window
that I lean out of to watch
the street lamps going out.

Through the ashes of the streets shadows
cross leaving no trace; men who pass by,
who don't come to me or stay in me,
carrying their solitary souls on their backs.

Daylight flees toward the west.
Night air approaches;
a bitter and confused fear,
almost pain, scarcely hope, arrives.

Everything that joined me to life
ceases to be, becomes distance,
goes farther off, finally disappears.
I am dead,
    . . . and no one lifts me up.

Miro
mi mano. Ésta que tantas veces
olvido
sobre los objetos
más ínfimos.
Ahora es como un pájaro
bruscamente caído
desde mi cuerpo hasta
ese sitio.
Otro hallazgo: aquí está
mi cuerpo. Vivo
en él sin saber
de él, casi sin sentirlo.
A veces tropieza
de improviso
contra otro cuerpo inevitable.
Y es el amor. Sorprendido,
lo siento entonces aislado,
entero, distinto.
Otras veces el sol
le dibuja un tibio
perfil, o el viento lo rodea
de un límite ceñido
y concreto.
Pero ahora es un frío
presentimiento.
¡Árbol erguido
frente a mí, súbito cuerpo
mío!
La sangre lo recorre. ¡Cómo
desciende! Oídlo:
éste es el corazón. Aquí se duerme
el pulso, igual que un río
en un remanso.

I look at
my hand. This one I so often
forget
on the most insignificant of
objects.
Now it's like a bird
suddenly fallen
from my body
down to this place.
Another discovery: here is
my body. I live
inside it without realizing,
almost without feeling.
Unexpectedly, at times,
it stumbles
against another inevitable body.
And that's love. Surprised,
I then feel isolated,
whole, distinct.
At other times the sun
draws it in tepid
profile, or the wind surrounds it
in a tight and concrete
circle.
But now there's a cold
premonition.
Like an erect tree
in front of me, sudden body
of mine!
The blood travels through it. How
it falls! Listen to it:
this is my heart. My pulse
sleeps here,
like a river eddy.

Allí está el limpio
hueso blanco en su cauce. La piel.
Los largos músculos tenaces y escondidos.
Sobre la tierra está. Sobre la tierra:
alta espiga de trigo,
joven álamo verde, viejo
olivo.
Está sobre la tierra. Estaba.
Yo lo he visto.
Un momento tan sólo.
                      . . . Su estatura
entre yo y esos campos amarillos.

This is the clean
white bone in its riverbed. The skin.
The muscles long, tenacious, concealed.
It's upon the earth. Over the earth:
tall ear of wheat,
green, young poplar, old
olive tree.
It's over the earth. It was.
I saw it.
For just a moment.

      . . . It stood tall
between me and those yellow fields.

Vengo de guerrear.
De guerrear por campos
de Castilla.
Cansado
de cabalgar.
Caballo, caballo
mío: descansa.
Ya es tiempo de enamorar
bajo los tilos que marzo
ilumina.

(Me voy soñando. Vengo de soñar.)

I COME FROM WAR

I come from war.
From battling through the fields
of Castile.
I'm tired
of riding.
Horse, my
horse: rest.
It's already time to fall in love
under the lime trees that March
illuminates.

(I go dreaming. I come from dream.)

Tras la ventana, el amor
vestido de blanco, mira.
Mira a la tarde, que gira
sus luces y su color.

La begonia sin olor
sus verdes hojas estira
para mirar lo que mira
tras la ventana, el amor:
la primavera, surgida
del pico de un ruiseñor.

LOVE DRESSED IN WHITE

Behind the window, love,
dressed in white, looks on.
It watches the afternoon that rotates
its lights and colors.

The scentless begonia
stretches its green leaves
to see what it sees
behind the window, love:
spring emerges
from the beak of the nightingale.

GEOGRAFÍA HUMANA

Lúbrica polinesia de lunares
en la pulida mar de tu cadera.
Trópico del tabaco y la madera
mecido por las olas de tus mares.

En los helados círculos polares
toda tu superficie reverbera . . .
Bajo las luces de tu primavera,
a punto de deshielo, los glaciares.

Los salmones avanzan por tus venas
meridianos rompiendo en su locura.
Las aves vuelan desde tus colinas.

Terreno fértil, huerto de azucenas:
tan variada riqueza de hermosura
pesa sobre tus hombros, que te inclinas.

HUMAN GEOGRAPHY

Lascivious polynesia of beauty marks
in the polished sea of your hips.
Tropic of tobacco and wood
rocked by the waves of your seas.

In the frozen polar circles
all of your surfaces reverberate . . .
Under the lights of your spring,
to the point of thawing, the glaciers.

Salmon swim through your veins,
breaking meridians in their madness.
Birds fly from your hills.

Fertile earth, garden of white lilies:
such varied riches of beauty
weigh on your shoulders, that you incline.

SONETO A ALGUNOS POETAS

Todas vuestras palabras son oscuras.
Avanzáis hacia el hombre con serena
palidez: miedo trágico que os llena
la boca de palabras más bien puras.

Decís palabras sórdidas y duras:
fusil, muchacha, dolorido, hiena.
Lloráis a veces. Honda es vuestra pena.
Oscura, inútil, triste entre basuras.

España es una plaza provinciana
y en ella pregonáis la mercancía:
un niño muerto por una azucena.

Nadie se para a oíros. Y mañana
proseguiréis llorando. Día a día.
. . . Impura, inútil, honda es vuestra pena.

TO SOME POETS

All of your words are obscure.
You advance towards the man with serene
pallor: tragic fear fills
your mouth with words more pure.

You say words that are sordid and lasting:
rifle, girl, grief-stricken, hyena.
You sometimes weep. Your pain is so very deep.
Obscure, useless, sadness among the refuse.

Spain is a provincial plaza
in her announcements of merchandise:
a dead child by a tiger lily.

No one hears you. And tomorrow
you will go on crying. Day by day.
. . . Impure, useless, your deep pain.

Por aquí pasa un río.
Por aquí tus pisadas
fueron embelleciendo las arenas,
aclarando las aguas,
puliendo los guijarros, perdonando
a las embelesadas
azucenas . . .

No vas tú por el río:
es el río el que anda
detrás de ti, buscando en ti
el reflejo, mirándose en tu espalda.

Si vas de prisa, el río se apresura.
Si vas despacio, el agua se remansa.

THROUGH HERE A RIVER PASSES

Through here a river passes.
Through here your footsteps
went embellishing the sands,
brightening the waters,
polishing the pebbles, forgiving
the enraptured
lilies . . .

It's not you who follows the river:
it's the river that flows
after you, seeking its reflection
in you, gazing at itself in your back.

If you walk swiftly, the river quickens.
If you walk slowly, the water forms a pool.

El otoño cruzaba
las colinas de débiles
temblores. Cada
hoja caída
estremecía toda una montaña.

Leve rumor de luces y de brisas
rodaba por el valle, se acercaba.
Los pájaros dejaban bruscamente
temblorosas las ramas
cayéndose hacia el cielo, arrebatados
por una fuerza extraña.
Las carnosas ortigas
se apretaban
como un rebaño
inquieto. Levantaban del agua
su cabeza, los juncos.
Las verdinegras zarzas
se crecían.
Imperceptibles, más delgadas
por la tensa postura de su espera,
las hierbas, anhelantes . . .

                Tú llegabas,
y una amarilla paz de hojas caídas
reponía el silencio a tus espaldas.

AUTUMN SENT

Autumn sent
slight shivers through
the hills. Each
fallen leaf started
an entire mountain trembling.

A faint murmur of lights and breezes
rolled through the valley, came closer.
Birds left branches
trembling and suddenly
swooped toward the sky, snatched up
by some strange force.
Plump nettles
huddled
like an uneasy
flock. Reeds raised their heads
from the water.
Dark-green brambles
swelled.
Imperceptible, more slender,
in the rigid posture of their waiting,
the grasses, longing . . .

　　　　　　　You were coming,
a yellow truce of fallen leaves
restoring silence at your back.

Perros contra la luna, lejanísimos,
llevan hasta los ámbitos
más próximos la inquietud de la noche
rumorosa. Claros
sonidos, antes inaudibles,
se perciben ahora. Ecos vagos,
jirones de palabras, goznes
agrios,
desasosiegan el recinto en sombra.

Apenas sin espacio,
el silencio, el inasible
silencio, cercado
por los ruidos, se aprieta
en torno de tus piernas y tus brazos,
asciende levemente a tu cabeza
y cae por tus cabellos destrenzados.

Es la noche y el sueño: no te inquietes.
El silencio ha crecido como un árbol.

DOGS AGAINST THE MOON

Dogs against the moon, very far away,
bring closer
the restlessness of the murmuring
night. Clear
sounds, once inaudible,
are now heard. Vague echoes,
shreds of words, creaking
hinges,
disturb the shadowed circle.

Scarcely without space,
the silence, the silence
you can't hold, closed in
by sounds, presses
against your arms and legs,
rises gently to your head,
and falls through your loosened hair.

It's night and the dream: don't be uneasy.
The silence has grown like a tree.

Milagro de la luz: la sombra nace,
choca en silencio contra las montañas,
se desploma sin peso sobre el suelo
desvelando a las hierbas delicadas.
Los eucaliptos dejan en la tierra
la temblorosa piel de su alargada
silueta, en la que vuelan fríos
pájaros que no cantan.
Una sombra más leve y más sencilla,
que nace de tus piernas, se adelanta
para anunciar el último, el más puro
milagro de la luz: tú contra el alba.

MIRACLE OF THE LIGHT

Miracle of the light: the shadow is born,
it strikes in silence against the mountains,
tumbles weightlessly to the ground,
keeping the delicate grasses awake.
The eucalyptus trees leave upon the earth
the trembling bark of their lengthened
silhouette, over which fly cold
birds that do not sing.
A slighter and simpler shadow,
born from your legs, comes forward
to announce the ultimate, the purest
miracle of the light: you against the dawn.

CIUDAD

Brillan las cosas. Los tejados crecen
sobre las copas de los árboles.
A punto de romperse, tensas,
las elásticas calles.
Ahí estás tú: debajo de ese cruce
de metálicos cables,
en el que cuaja el sol como en un nimbo
complementario de tu imagen.
Rápidas golondrinas amenazan
fachadas impasibles. Los cristales
transmiten luminosos y secretos
mensajes.
Todo son breves gestos, invisibles
para los ojos habituales.
Y de pronto, no estás. Adiós, amor, adiós.
Ya te marchaste.
Nada queda de ti. La ciudad gira:
molino en el que todo se deshace.

CITY

Things glisten. Roof tiles rise
over the tree tops.
Almost to the breaking point, tense,
the resilient streets.
There you are: beneath the intersection
of metallic cables,
where the sun fits like a halo
complimenting your image.
Rapid swallows threaten
impassive facades. Glass
transmits luminous and secretive
messages.
Everything consists of brief, invisible
gestures for habitual eyes.
And suddenly you're not there. Good-bye, love, good-bye.
You're already gone.
Nothing remains of you. The city rotates:
grinder in which everything is undone.

SIN ESPERANZA CON CONVENCIMIENTO

1961

WITHOUT HOPE, BUT WITH CONVICTION

1961

EL DERROTADO

Atrás quedaron los escombros:
humeantes pedazos de tu casa,
veranos incendiados, sangre seca
sobre la que se ceba—último buitre—
el viento.

Tú emprendes viaje hacia adelante, hacia
el tiempo bien llamado porvenir.
Porque ninguna tierra
posees,
porque ninguna patria
es ni será jamás la tuya,
porque en ningún país
puede arraigar tu corazón deshabitado.

Nunca—y es tan sencillo—
podrás abrir una cancela
y decir, nada más: *buen día,*
madre.
Aunque efectivamente el día sea bueno,
haya trigo en las eras
y los árboles
extiendan hacia ti sus fatigadas
ramas, ofreciéndote
frutos o sombra para que descanses.

THE DEFEATED ONE

Left behind was wreckage:
the smoking remains of your house,
summers set on fire, dried blood
upon which the wind—that ultimate vulture—
feeds.

You begin a journey forward, toward
the time appropriately called "the future."
Because you own
no piece of earth,
because no country
is or ever will be yours,
because in no land
can your deserted heart take root.

Never—and it's so simple—
will you be able to open the gate
and simply say: *Good morning,*
mother.
Even though the morning really is a good one,
and there's wheat on the threshing-room floor,
and trees,
their weary
branches extending, offering
fruits or shade in which you can rest.

Mundo asombroso
surge bruscamente.

Me da miedo la luna
embalsamada
en las aguas del río,
el bosque silencioso
que araña con sus ramas
el vientre de la lluvia,
los pájaros
que aúllan en el túnel de la noche
y todo
lo que súbitamente
hace un gesto y sonríe
para marchar de pronto.

En medio
de la cruel retirada de las cosas
precipitándose en desorden hacia
la nada y la ceniza,
mi corazón naufraga en la zozobra
del destino del mundo que lo cerca.
¿A dónde va ese viento y esa luz,
el grito
de la roja amapola inesperada,
el canto de las grises
gaviotas de los puertos?

¿Y qué ejército es ese que me lleva
envuelto en su derrota y en su huida
—fatigado rehén, yo, prisionero
sin número y sin nombre, maniatado
entre escuadras de gritos fugitivos—
hacia la sombra donde van las luces,
hacia el silencio donde la voz muere?

ASTONISHING WORLD

An astonishing world
suddenly looms up.

I'm afraid of the moon
embalmed
in the waters of the river,
the silent forest
that scratches with its branches
the belly of the rain,
birds
that howl in the tunnel of night
and everything
that unexpectedly
makes a gesture and smiles
only to suddenly disappear.

In the midst
of the cruel retreat of things
rushing in headlong flight toward
nothingness and ashes,
my heart goes under in the shipwreck
of the fate of the world that surrounds it.
Where does the wind go, that light,
the cry
of the unexpected red poppy,
the singing of the gray
sea gulls of the ports?

And what army is it that takes me
wrapped up in its defeat and its flight
—I, a prisoner, a weary hostage,
without name or number, handcuffed
among squads of fugitive cries—
toward the shadows where the lights go,
toward the silence where my voice dies.

EL CAMPO DE BATALLA

Hoy voy a describir el campo
de batalla
tal como yo lo vi, una vez decidida
la suerte de los hombres que lucharon
muchos hasta morir,
otros
hasta seguir viviendo todavía.

No hubo elección:
murió quien pudo,
quien no pudo morir continuó andando,
los árboles nevaban lentos frutos,
era verano, invierno, todo un año
o más quizá: era la vida
entera
aquel enorme día de combate.

Por el oeste el viento traía sangre,
por el este la tierra era ceniza,
el norte entero estaba
bloqueado
por alambradas secas y por gritos,
y únicamente el sur,
tan sólo
el sur,
se ofrecía ancho y libre a nuestros ojos.

Pero el sur no existía:
ni agua, ni luz, ni sombra, ni ceniza
llenaban su oquedad, su hondo vacío:
el sur era un enorme precipicio,
un abismo sin fin de donde,
lentos,
los poderosos buitres ascendían.

THE BATTLEFIELD

Today I'm going to tell you about
the battlefield
just as I saw it. It was a time that decided
the fate of thousands of men who fought
to the death,
others
who continue living still.

There was no choice:
whoever could, died;
whoever couldn't, kept on going;
the trees slowly snowed fruit,
it was summer, winter, a whole year,
or perhaps more: it was an entire
lifetime
that tremendous day of fighting.

From the west the wind brought blood,
to the east the earth was ashes,
the entire north was
blockaded
by withered barbed wire and shouts,
and only the south,
just
the south,
offered itself free and wide to our eyes.

But the south didn't exist:
neither water, nor light, nor shadow, nor ashes
filled its emptiness, its deep hollowness:
the south was a lofty cliff,
an endless abyss from where,
slowly,
the ponderous vultures ascended.

Nadie escuchó la voz del capitán
porque tampoco el capitán hablaba.
Nadie enterró a los muertos.
Nadie dijo:
dale a mi novia esto si la encuentras
un día.

Tan sólo alguien remató a un caballo
que, con el vientre abierto,
agonizante,
llenaba con su espanto el aire en sombra:
el aire que la noche amenazaba.

Quietos, pegados a la dura
tierra,
cogidos entre el pánico y la nada,
los hombres esperaban el momento
último,
sin oponerse ya,
sin rebeldía.

Algunos se murieron,
como dije,
y los demás, tendidos, derribados,
pegados a la tierra en paz al fin,
esperan
ya no sé qué
—quizá que alguien les diga:
amigos, podéis iros, el combate . . .

Entre tanto,
es verano otra vez,
y crece el trigo
en el que fue ancho campo de batalla.

No one heard the voice of the captain
because the captain was silent.
No one buried the dead.
No one said:
*Give this to my sweetheart if you meet her
one day.*

Someone just finished off a horse
that, with its belly split open,
and in agony,
filled the shadowy air with terror:
air that the night threatened.

Quietly, pinned to the hard
earth,
caught between panic and nothingness,
the men waited for the last
moment,
already defeated,
with acceptance.

As I said,
some of them died,
and the rest, lying there, struck down,
pinned to the earth in peace at last,
waited,
I don't know what for
—perhaps for someone to tell them:
Friend, you can leave now, the fighting . . .

Meanwhile
it's summer again
and the wheat flourishes
on what was once a battlefield.

Esperanza,
araña negra del atardecer.
Te paras
no lejos de mi cuerpo
abandonado, andas
en torno a mí,
tejiendo, rápida,
inconsistentes hilos invisibles,
te acercas, obstinada,
y me acaricias casi con tu sombra
pesada
y leve a un tiempo.

Agazapada
bajo las piedras y las horas,
esperaste, paciente, la llegada
de esta tarde
en la que nada
es ya posible . . .
                    Mi corazón:
tu nido.
          Muerde en él, esperanza.

HOPE

Hope,
black spider of twilight.
You stop
not far from my abandoned
body, walk
around me,
swiftly weaving,
invisible, flimsy threads,
obstinately, you come closer,
you almost brush me with your shadow,
heavy and light
at the same time.

Crouching
beneath stones and hours,
you waited, patiently, for the arrival
of this evening
in which nothing
is now possible . . .
　　　　　　　My heart:
your nest.
　　　　　Bite into it, hope.

DE DOS PALABRAS NÍTIDAS AHORA

A Vicente Aleixandre,
por su libro La destrucción o el amor

Destruirse o amar . . . ¿Qué significa
esa cruel disyuntiva o amenaza,
ese pavor cuyo final aplaza
la incertidumbre? ¿Opone o identifica

lo que enlaza? La voz que nos lo explica
señala, desmenuza, despedaza,
profundiza en el ser, mas no desplaza
el misterio que el verbo intensifica.

Es difícil saber. Pero yo intuyo
esa verdad oscura, consecuencia
de dos palabras nítidas ahora:

ruina total, o fuego igual que el tuyo.
Dilema sin salida: no existencia,
o vida incendio que el amor devora.

OF TWO WORDS NOW MADE CLEAR

To Vicente Aleixandre,
for his book Destruction Or Love

To self-destruct or to love . . . What does it mean
that cruel dilemma or threat,
terror whose end postpones
this uncertainty? Does it oppose or identify

what it binds together? The voice that explains it to us
names, shreds, tears it apart,
penetrates its being but doesn't upset
the mystery the verb intensifies.

It's hard to know. But I sense
one obscure truth, the consequence
of two words now made clear:

total ruin, or a fire the same as yours.
Dilemma without escape: nonexistence
or a life-fire that love devours.

AYER

Ayer fue miércoles toda la mañana.
Por la tarde cambió:
se puso casi lunes,
la tristeza invadió los corazones
y hubo un claro
movimiento de pánico hacia los
tranvías
que llevan los bañistas hasta el río.

A eso de las siete cruzó el cielo
una lenta avioneta, y ni los niños
la miraron.
        Se desató
el frío,
alguien salió a la calle con sombrero,
ayer, y todo el día
fue igual,
ya veis,
qué divertido,
ayer y siempre ayer y así hasta ahora,
continuamente andando por las calles
gente desconocida,
o bien dentro de casa merendando
pan y café con leche, ¡qué
alegría!

La noche vino pronto y se encendieron
amarillos y cálidos faroles,
y nadie pudo
impedir que al final amaneciese
el día de hoy,
tan parecido
pero
¡tan diferente en luces y en aroma!

YESTERDAY

Yesterday was Wednesday all morning.
By afternoon it changed:
it became almost Monday,
sadness invaded hearts
and there was a distinct
panic of movement toward
the trolleys
that take the swimmers down to the river.

At about seven a small plane slowly
crossed the sky, but not even the children
watched it.
         The cold
was unleashed,
someone went outdoors wearing a hat,
yesterday, and the whole day
was like that,
already you see,
how amusing,
yesterday and always yesterday and even now,
strangers
are constantly walking through the streets
or happily indoors snacking on
bread and coffee with cream: what
joy!

Night fell suddenly,
the warm yellow street lamps were lit,
and no one could
impede the final dawn
of today's day,
so similar
and yet
so different in lights and aroma!

Por eso mismo,
porque es como os digo,
dejadme que os hable
de ayer, una vez más
de ayer: el día
incomparable que ya nadie nunca
volverá a ver jamás sobre la tierra.

For that very same reason,
because everything is just as I told you,
let me tell you
about yesterday, once more
about yesterday: the incomparable
day that no one will ever
see again upon the earth.

DOMINGO

Domingo, flor de luz, casi increíble
día. Bajas sobre la tierra
como un ángel inútil y dorado.
Besas
a las muchachas
de turbia cabellera,
vistes de azul marino
a los hombres que te aman, y dejas
en las manos del niño
un aro de madera
o una simple esperanza. Repartes
golondrinas, globos de primavera,
te subes a las torres
y giras las veletas
oxidadas. Tu viento agita faldas
de colores, estremece banderas,
lleva lejos canciones
y sonrisas, y llena
las estancias de polvo plateado.
Los árboles esperan
tu llegada
para cubrirse de gorriones. Sabe más fresca
el agua de las fuentes.
Las campanas dispersan
palomas imprevistas
que vuelan
de otro modo.
No hay nadie que no sepa
que es domingo,
domingo.
          Tu presencia
de espuma lava,
eleva,
hace flotar las cosas y los seres

SUNDAY

Sunday, flower of light, almost unbelievable
day. You descend upon the earth
like a useless golden angel.
You kiss
the girls
with windblown hair,
dress in navy blue
the men who love you, and leave
in the children's hands
a wooden ring
or a simple hope. You hand out
swallows, spring balloons,
and climb towers
to spin the rusty
weather vanes. Your wind ruffles
brightly colored skirts, ripples flags,
carries away songs
and smiles, and fills
rooms with a silvery dust.
Trees await
your arrival
to cover themselves with sparrows. The water
from the fountains tastes the freshest.
Bells disperse
unexpected doves
that fly
away.
There's no one who doesn't know
it's Sunday,
Sunday.
        Your foamy
presence washes,
lifts,
floats things and beings

en un nítido cielo que no era
—el lunes—de verdad:
apenas
desteñido papel, vidrio olvidado,
polvo tedioso sobre las aceras . . .

in a spotless sky that was
—on Monday—not real:
scarcely
faded paper, forgotten glass,
tedious dust upon the sidewalks . . .

EL INVIERNO

El invierno
de lunas anchas y pequeños días
está sobre nosotros. Hace tiempo
yo era niño y nevaba mucho,
mucho. Lo recuerdo
viendo a la tierra negra que reposa,
apenas por el hielo
de un charco iluminada.
Es increíble: pero todo esto
que hoy es tierra dormida bajo el frío,
será mañana, bajo el viento,
trigo.
     Y rojas
amapolas. Y sarmientos . . .

Sin esperanza:
la tierra de Castilla está esperando
—crecen los ríos—
con convencimiento.

WINTER

The winter
of broad moons and small days
is upon us. A long time ago
I was a boy and it snowed
and snowed. I remember it,
staring at the black earth at rest,
barely illuminated
by the ice of a pond.
It's incredible: but all of this
earth sleeping beneath the cold today
will be wheat tomorrow,
in the wind.
          And red
poppies. And vine shoots . . .

Without hope: .
the land of Castile is waiting
—the rivers are rising—
with conviction.

EL FUTURO

Pero el futuro es diferente
al porvenir que se adivina lejos,
terreno mágico, dilatada esfera
que el largo brazo del deseo roza,
bola brillante que los ojos sueñan,
compartida estancia
de la esperanza y de la decepción, oscura
patria
de la ilusión y el llanto
que los astros predicen
y el corazón espera
y siempre, siempre, siempre está distante.

Pero el futuro es otra cosa, pienso:
tiempo de verbo en marcha, acción, combate,
movimiento buscado hacia la vida,
quilla de barco que golpea el agua
y se esfuerza en abrir entre las olas
la brecha exacta que el timón ordena.

En esa línea estoy, en esa honda
trayectoria de lucha y agonía,
contenido en el túnel o trinchera
que con mis manos abro, cierro, o dejo,
obedeciendo al corazón, que manda,
empuja, determina, exige, busca.

¡Futuro mío . . . ! Corazón lejano
que lo dictaste ayer:
no te avergüences.
Hoy es el resultado de tu sangre,
dolor que reconozco, luz que admito,

THE FUTURE

But the future is different
from that destiny seen from afar,
magical world, vast sphere
brushed by the long arm of desire,
brilliant ball the eyes dream,
shared dwelling
of hope and deception, dark
land
of illusion and tears
the stars predicted
and the heart awaits
and that is always, always, always distant.

But, I think, the future is also another thing:
a verb tense in motion, in action, in combat,
a searching movement toward life,
keel of the ship that strikes the water
and struggles to open between the waves
the exact breach the rudder commands.

I'm on this line, in this deep
trajectory of agony and battle,
trapped in a tunnel or trench
that with my hands I open, close, or leave,
obeying the heart that orders,
pushes, determines, demands, and searches.

Future of mine . . . ! Distant heart
that dictated it yesterday:
don't be ashamed.
Today is the result of your blood,
pain that I recognize, light that I admit,

sufrimiento que asumo,
amor que intento.

Pero nada es aún definitivo.
Mañana he decidido ir adelante,
y avanzaré,
mañana me dispongo a estar contento,
mañana te amaré, mañana
y tarde,
mañana no será lo que Dios quiera.

Mañana gris, o luminosa, o fría,
que unas manos modelan en el viento,
que unos puños dibujan en el aire.

suffering that I assume,
love that I intend.

But still, nothing is definitive.
Tomorrow I have decided to go ahead
and advance,
tomorrow I am prepared to be content,
tomorrow I will love you, morning
and night,
tomorrow will not be exactly as God wishes.

Tomorrow, gray or luminous, or cold,
that hands shape in the wind,
that fists draw in the air.

CUMPLEAÑOS DE AMOR

¿Cómo seré yo
cuando no sea yo?
Cuando el tiempo
haya modificado mi estructura,
y mi cuerpo sea otro,
otra mi sangre,
otros mis ojos y otros mis cabellos.
Pensaré en ti, tal vez.
Seguramente,
mis sucesivos cuerpos
—prolongándome, vivo, hacia la muerte—
se pasarán de mano en mano,
de corazón a corazón,
de carne a carne,
el elemento misterioso
que determina mi tristeza
cuando te vas,
que me impulsa a buscarte ciegamente,
que me lleva a tu lado
sin remedio:
lo que la gente llama amor, en suma.
Y los ojos
—qué importa que no sean estos ojos—
te seguirán a donde vayas, fieles.

THE BIRTHDAY OF LOVE

What will I be like
when I'm not myself?
When time
has changed my body
and it's become another body,
my blood another's blood,
my eyes other eyes, and my hair another's hair.
Perhaps I'll think of you.
Surely
my successive bodies
—prolonging me, my life, until death comes—
will pass from hand to hand,
from heart to heart,
from flesh to flesh,
that mysterious element
that determines my sadness
when you go away,
that drives me to seek you blindly,
that takes me inevitably
to your side:
in other words, what everyone calls love.
And my eyes
—what does it matter that they will not be these eyes—
will follow you faithfully wherever you go.

DICIEMBRE

Diciembre vino silenciosamente,
estirando las noches hasta casi
juntarlas:
el alba a pocas horas de distancia
del crepúsculo lleno de tristeza,
y un mediodía sin sol,
un mediodía
de pájaros ocultos y apagados
ruidos,
con bajas nubes grises recibiendo
el sucio impacto de las chimeneas.

Diciembre vino así, como lo cuento
aquel año de gracia del que hablo,
el año aquel de gracia y sueño, leve
soplo de luces y de días,
encrucijada luminosa
de lunas hondas y de estrellas altas,
de mañanas de sol, de tardes tibias
que por el aire se sucedían lentas
corno globos brillantes y solemnes.

Pero diciembre vino de ese modo
y cubrió todo aquello de ceniza:
lluvia turbia y menuda,
niebla densa,
opaca luz borrando los perfiles,
espeso frío tenaz que vaciaba
las calles de muchachas
y de música,

DECEMBER

December came silently,
stretching the nights out until they almost
touched:
dawn just a few hours away
from a twilight filled with sadness,
and a sunless noon,
a noon
of hidden birds and muffled
sounds,
with low gray clouds absorbing
the filthy smoke from chimneys.

As I said, December came just like that,
in that year of grace I speak of,
that year of grace and dreams, a slight
breath of lights and days,
a luminous crossroads
of low moons and lofty stars,
sunny mornings, warm afternoons
that followed one another through the air,
as slow and dignified as shiny balloons.

But December came
and covered everything with ash:
dingy drizzle,
dense fog,
opaque light blurring the outlines,
thick stubborn cold that emptied
the streets of young girls
and music,

que asesinaba pájaros y mármoles
en la ciudad sin hojas del invierno.

Pájaros muertos, barro, nieve sucia,
lanzó diciembre sobre el año, y todos
abandonamos en silencio
su ámbito feliz, pisando indiferentes
los restos consumidos de sus cosas,
el envoltorio de sus alegrías,
dejándolo cubierto de papeles
y rotas luces,
oquedad sumergida
en decepción y desfallecimiento,
como la sala de un teatro, cuando
el telón cae, finalizado el drama.

De esa forma dejamos aquel año,
sórdido
recinto
manchado de recuerdos derribados
y deseos oscuros
y nostalgia
—y por qué no también remordimiento—
sin mirar para atrás,
sin querer enterarnos
de su agonía lívida a las puertas de enero.

that murdered birds and statues
in the leafless winter city.

December cast upon the year
dead birds, mud, dirty snow, and we all
abandoned in silence
its happy confines, treading indifferently
upon the wasted remains of its possessions,
the bundle of its joys,
leaving it covered with papers
and broken lights,
hollowness sunken
in disillusion and languor,
like a theater, when
the curtain falls, and the play is over.

That's how we left that year,
sordid
enclosure
stained with demolished memories
and dark desires
and nostalgia
—and why not also remorse—
without looking back,
without wanting to know
its livid agony at the gates of January.

CARTA SIN DESPEDIDA

A veces,
mi egoísmo me llena
de maldad
y te odio casi
hasta hacerme daño
a mí mismo:
son los celos, la envidia,
el asco
al hombre, mi semejante
aborrecible, como yo
corrompido y sin remedio,
mi querido
hermano y parigual en la desgracia.

A veces—o mejor dicho:
casi nunca—,
te odio tanto que te veo distinta.
Ni en corazón ni en alma te pareces
a la que amaba sólo hace un instante
y hasta tu cuerpo cambia
y es más bello
—quizá por imposible y por lejano.

Pero el odio también me modifica
a mí mismo,
y cuando quiero darme cuenta
soy otro
que no odia,
que ama
a esa desconocida cuyo nombre es el tuyo,
que lleva tu apellido,
y tiene,

LETTER WITHOUT GOOD-BYE

At times,
my egotism fills me
with evil,
and I hate you so much
that I almost do harm
to myself:
it's jealousy, envy,
disgust
for man, my abhorrent
fellow man, who is just like me,
corrupt and hopeless,
my beloved
brother and equal in misfortune.

At times—or rather:
once in a while—,
I hate you so much that I see you as a different person.
Neither in heart nor soul do you resemble
the person I loved just a moment ago,
and even your body changes
and becomes more beautiful
—perhaps because it's distant and unattainable.

But hatred also changes
me,
and before I realize it
I am someone else
who doesn't hate,
who loves
that unknown woman with your first name,
with your last name,
and who,

igual que tú,
largo el cabello.

Cuando sonríes, yo te reconozco,
identifico tu perfil primero,
y vuelvo a verte,
al fin,
tal como eras, como sigues
siendo,
como serás ya siempre, mientras te ame.

just like you,
wears her hair long.

I recognize your profile first,
I recognize you when you smile,
and I see you again,
at last,
just as you were, as you go on
being,
as you will always be, as long as I love you.

SÍMBOLO

Símbolo,
oscuro disfraz
del destino.

Ocho quiere decir:
                    Amor.
Nueve, ¡quién sabe!
Sería preciso
dejar de ser
hombre. Pero
es sabido
—y a todo el mundo consta—
que detrás del color
amarillo
se oculta una traición:
la más frecuente. ¡Cuidado!
Engañan las palabras,
las cifras, los sonidos.
Nada es lo que parece.
El peligro
está detrás de todo.
Hará falta moverse
con mucho
sigilo
para no tropezar
con el hierro
que nos desgarraría el alma fatalmente.
El secreto es sencillo:
confianza y desconfianza, olvidar
lo aprendido,
cerrar los ojos si
lo evidente se ensaña
con nosotros, pronunciar las palabras
elementales, llorar

SYMBOL

Symbol,
destiny's
dark disguise.

Eight means:
                    love.
Nine, who knows!
One would have
to stop being
a man. But
it's known
—and clear to everyone—
that treachery lies
behind
the color yellow:
the most frequent one. Beware!
Words deceive,
figures, sounds.
Nothing is what it seems to be.
Danger
lies behind everything.
We would need to move
with a great deal
of stealth
so as not to stumble
upon the weapon
that would fatally slash our soul.
The secret is so simple:
trust and mistrust, forget
what has been learned,
close our eyes if
the obvious enrages
us, say the simple
words, weep

de cuando en cuando, vivir como si nada
hubiese sucedido.

El agua clara significa: espera.
Restos de luz en el atardecer: olvido.

from time to time, live as if nothing
had happened.

Clear water signifies: waiting.
Glimmers of light at dusk: oblivion.

PASTOR DE VIENTOS

Pastor de vientos, desde
los infinitos horizontes
acuden los rebaños a tus manos.
Seguro el porvenir, miras el ancho
paisaje de colinas, esperando
la brisa que te traiga
aquel aroma dócil a tomillo
o el hondo olor a bosque del invierno.
La lluvia viene luego, infatigable,
y se acuesta a tus pies formando charcos
que emigran hacia el cielo en el verano.
Y por el aire bajan
pájaros y perfumes, hojas secas,
mil cosas
que tú dejas o guardas con mirada profunda.
Cada día te trae una sorpresa,
y tú cantas,
pastor,
cantas o silbas
a las altas estrellas también tuyas.

SHEPHERD OF WINDS

Shepherd of winds, from
the infinite horizons
the herds come to meet your hands.
Future secured, you watch the broad
landscape of hills, waiting
for the breeze to bring
the docile aroma of thyme
or the smell of deep winter forests.
Later, the restless rains come
to lie at your feet in pools
that emigrate to the sky in summer.
And through the air descend
birds and smells, dry leaves,
a thousand things
you leave or protect with a profound gaze.
Each day brings surprise,
and you sing,
Shepherd,
you sing or whistle
to the highest stars, also yours.

GRADO ELEMENTAL

1962

ELEMENTARY GRADE

1962

LECCIONES DE COSAS

Por encima del campo pasó el mes de septiembre.
Quizá el último sol del otoño
—antes de que las lluvias
lleguen—sea este
sol en periplo rápido (entre rosadas nubes)
hacia
su lejano destino, arrebatado
de todos los espacios
por la ciega atracción de otro cuerpo celeste.
(Consúltense estos nombres en una enciclopedia:
galaxia, paralaje, azimut, Newton, auge.)

De cualquier forma, no es preciso
mirar hacia lo alto para maravillarse.
Sorteando las—para ellas—corpulentas
briznas de hierba,
más cerca de la tierra aún que nosotros,
he aquí a las hormigas
(*Hormigas*: insectos himenópteros que viven
asociados. Véase también: *abejas.*)
esforzándose
por llevar otro grano a su granero.
Conscientes—me parece—
de la proximidad de la estación lluviosa,
intensifican
su actividad, con intención, sin duda,
de aprovechar al máximo el tiempo que les queda.

Imitémoslas.

Pero como los días
son cortos (el sol se pone
hacia las diecisiete y treinta y cinco,
y la luna,

LESSONS OF THINGS

September flew over the countryside.
Perhaps the last autumn sun
—before the rains
come—will be this
sun in its swift journey (through pink clouds)
toward
its distant fate, stolen
from all of space
by the blind attraction of another celestial body.
(Consult an encyclopedia for the following:
galaxy, parallax, azimuth, Newton, meridian.)

Anyway, one need not
look up to marvel.
Sorting through—for them—thick
blades of grass,
closer to earth than even we are,
are the ants
(*Ants*: social hymenoptera.
See also: *bees.*)
struggling
with one more grain of earth for their nest.
Aware—it seems to me—
of the coming rainy season,
they intensify
their work, with every intention, no doubt,
of taking advantage of the time that's left.

Let's be like them.

But since the days
are short (the sun sets
by five thirty-five,
and the moon,

aunque llena hoy y en Libra,
no brillará en el cielo hasta muy tarde)
utilicemos
la última luz para llenar los ojos
con tanta realidad abrumadora:

cosas que son y que no son,
como este río
distinto cada instante
a su inmediato próximo pasado
fluvial cadáver que en la mar descansa;
cosas que sobreviven en su forma
siempre provisional, mas sin embargo
tenazmente buscada,
igual que esa lejana cordillera
pulida por ventiscas y glaciares;
vidas que se desviven poco a poco
vivificando con su lenta muerte
nuevas muestras de flora y de paisaje.

Hostil y sometido,
entregado y violento,
éste es el escenario y el soporte
del hombre.

Aquí vivió su oscura,
su dolorosa infancia,
recién llegado apenas
a este recinto despiadado y húmedo,
invitado
del azar y de nadie,
inesperado huésped de los bosques,
usurpador del reino de las fieras
y de los ciegos, tercos vegetales,
fiera insaciable él mismo
que consiguió matar cuanto negaba

although full today and in Libra,
will not shine in the sky until much later)
let's use
that last light to fill the eyes
with an overwhelming reality:

things that are and are not,
like this river
every instant different
from its immediate, just past,
fluvial corpse that rests in the sea;
things that survive in its shape,
always provisional but just
as tenaciously sought
as that distant cordillera
polished by blizzards and glaciers;
lives that die little by little
nurturing with their slow deaths
new examples of flora and landscape.

Hostile and subjected,
surrendered and violent,
this is the scenario and support
of man.

Here he's lived his dark,
painful childhood,
arriving barely alive
at this unmerciful and humid place,
invited
by chance and nothing else,
unexpected guest of the forests,
usurper of the wild kingdom
of blind and stubborn vegetables,
the same insatiable beast
who manages to kill everything that desire

su deseo,
que supo rescatar de los incendios
el calor y la luz,
y oponer a los vientos las extensas
y blancas velas de las naves,
y detener o derramar las aguas
sobre la tierra exhausta y arañada,
mordida, rota, transformada, dócil
como un cuerpo vencido o disfrutado.

Ésta es, en fin, la clara piedra
donde su incierta historia queda escrita.
Y si a veces lo olvida,
si vuelve su mirada hacia otra parte
intentando extraer de lo ya abstracto
una idea concreta que lo explique,
todo es lo mismo ya.
                    Sucede entonces,
que si habla, el hombre, aunque no quiera, miente.

denies,
who learned to rescue from the blazing fires
light and warmth,
and to turn the vast white sails of ships
against the wind,
and to contain or scatter the waters
over the exhausted earth, scratched,
bitten, broken, transformed, docile
like a body defeated or enjoyed.

This, in short, is the clear stone
where his uncertain history remains written.
And if he should forget it,
if he turns his gaze elsewhere,
seeking to pull from the already abstract
a concrete idea that might explain it,
he'll find it's all the same now.
                              For it just so happens
that if he speaks, man, even when he doesn't mean to, lies.

ESTÍO EN BIDONVILLE

Languidez de las cosas subalternas,
inútiles objetos, olvidados,
grises
plataformas del polvo
cotidiano,
sucios cristales ante turbios cielos,
contra los que los gatos
mayan, duermen, se aburren,
paseando
su felino desdén, su desenfado
torvo, su angulosa
y erizada estructura, en el tejado
musgoso y apacible como
un prado.

Allí, en esa silla baja, es donde
el niño
      cojo
           se ha sentado
para ver las palomas . . .
—¿Qué palomas? No es cierto.
Yo estaba equivocado:
para ver
los papeles oscuros casi blancos
izados por el viento,
levantados
—lloverá—en un remedo
de vuelo sucio, inútil, fracasado.

Para ver a la cabra comeárboles
atada a un árbol carcomido y lacio,
para gustar el polvo en la saliva,
para oír a los grillos enjaulados
en su cárcel de alambre y de madera,

SUMMER IN SLUMVILLE

Torpor of trivial things,
useless objects, abandoned,
daily
heaps of gray
dust,
dirty windowpanes facing turbid skies,
against which the cats
meow, drowse, get bored,
prowling
their feline disdain, their fierce
unconcern, their angular
and bristling bodies, on the roof
which is as mossy and peaceful
as a meadow.

There, in that low chair, is where
the lame
      boy
         sat
to watch the doves . . .
—what doves? It's not clear.
I made a mistake:
to watch
the almost white papers
swept up by the wind,
lifted up
—it's going to rain—in a mockery
of dirty, useless, failed flight.

To see the tree-eating goat
staked to a withered worm-eaten tree,
to taste the dust in our saliva,
to hear the caged crickets
in their jails of wire and wood,

para cerrar los ojos deslumbrados
ante el destello súbito y violento
del sol en vidrios rotos reflejado,
para sentir las uñas de la tarde
clavándose en sus leves, blancos párpados,
y abrir después los ojos, y . . .

                              Silencio.
La ciudad rompe contra el campo
dejando en sus orillas amarillas,
en el polvo de hoy que será barro
luego,
los miserables restos de un naufragio
de colosales dimensiones: miles
de hombres sobreviven. Enseres y artefactos
—como ellos rotos, como ellos
oxidados—
flotan aquí y allá, o bien reposan
igual que ellos, salvados
hoy por hoy—¿sólo hoy?—, sobre esta tierra.

Mañana es un mar hondo que hay que cruzar a nado.

to close our dazzled eyes
before the sudden and violent flash
of sun reflected from broken windows,
to feel the fingernails of the afternoon
stabbing at our thin, white eyelids,
and then open our eyes afterwards, and . . .

                                        Silence.
The city breaks against the countryside,
leaving on its yellow shores,
in today's dust that will later be
mud,
the miserable refuse of a shipwreck
of colossal dimensions: thousands
of men survive. Furniture and junk
—like them broken, like them
rusted—
float here and there, or come to rest—
like them, saved
day by day—only today?—, upon this earth.

Tomorrow is a deep sea that will have to be crossed by swimming.

El momento no es bueno.
Ya se sabe
que los vientos tampoco.
Una tromba de agua arrasa a Cataluña.
La lluvia
no moja desde meses la tierra de Almería
Aquí, en cambio, los hielos ennegrecen
los frutos
y más allá los huracanes
derriban bosques, y en otro
lugar no tan lejano
un inmenso trigal fue pasto de las llamas.
No vamos a quejarnos por tan pequeña cosa.
No vamos a quejarnos desde ahora por nada.
Desde ahora
somos invulnerables de tanto vulnerados,
insensibles
de haber sentido tanto.
Y si un niño se muere o una ilusión se quiebra
no hay por qué preocuparse:
estamos
perfectamente disculpados.
Son los vientos, los tiempos, las desgracias que corren
como arañas hambrientas sobre nuestra inocencia.
Es el momento este que nos pesa en el pecho
igual que una gran piedra,
y nos inmoviliza.

En el aire quedaron vestigios de palabras:
— . . . *supervivientes todos de inclinada postura:*
sería
preferible
fallecer intentando enderezar los huesos . . . —
y pasó un aeroplano y ya no se oye nada.

THIS MOMENT

This moment is no good.
There's something
in the wind.
A whirlwind of water demolishes Catalonia.
Rain
hasn't moistened the earth of Almeria for months.
Here, however, ice blackens
the fruit
and over there hurricanes
knock down forests, and in another
place not so far away
an immense wheatfield was grazed by flames.
We don't weep over such small things.
We don't weep now for anything.
From now on
we're invulnerable because we've been hurt so often,
unfeeling
from having felt so much.
And if a child dies or an illusion cracks
there's nothing to worry about:
we are
perfectly exonerated.
These are the winds, the times, the misfortunes that run
over our innocence like hungry spiders.
It's this moment that weighs in the chest
like a huge stone,
and immobilizes us.

Vestiges of words remain in the air:
— . . . *survivors, all bowed down:*
it would be preferable
to die
trying to straighten out the bones . . . —
and then an airplane passes overhead, and now you can't hear anything.

Note: The quoted lines in italics are paraphrased from a speech made by Dolores Ibarruri, known as
"La Pasionaria," during the Spanish civil war.

PERLA DE LAS ANTILLAS

Ha estallado una perla, y las cenizas
de la libertad,
empujadas por el viento del Caribe,
siembran el desconcierto y el terror
entre los responsables de un continente inmenso.
Desde la Casa Blanca a la Rosada,
todos los techos de las Grandes Casas
están amenazados
por el irreparable, cruel desastre:
ha estallado una perla, y los residuos
de la dignidad
pueden contaminar a mucha gente.

Es preciso evitarlo, porque
si los indios que obtienen el estaño y el cobre
en las minas de Chile y de Bolivia,
si los habitantes de los suburbios de Buenos Aires
y los desposeídos del Perú,
si los oscuros buscadores de caucho
y los integrantes de las tribus de Paraguay y de Colombia,
si los analfabetos ciudadanos de Méjico
inscritos en el centro de electores y borrados del
              Registro de la propiedad,
si los que fertilizan con su sudor las plantaciones
de azúcar y café,
si los que recortan las pesadas selvas a golpe de machete
para incrementar la producción mundial de piñas en conserva,
si todos ellos y sus otros muchos
hermanos
en la desnutrición

PEARL OF THE ANTILLES

A pearl has exploded, and the ashes
of freedom,
propelled by the Caribbean wind,
sow chaos and terror
among those responsible for an immense continent.
From the White House to La Casa Rosada,
all the roofs of the Great Houses
are threatened
by a cruel, irreparable disaster:
a pearl has exploded, and the residue
of its dignity
could contaminate so many people.

It's necessary to avoid this, because
if the Indians who mine copper and tin
in the mines of Bolivia and Chile,
if the inhabitants of the outskirts of Buenos Aires
and the have-nots of Peru,
if the obscure rubber-tappers
and the indigenous tribes of Colombia and Paraguay,
if the illiterate citizens of Mexico
are registered in the Center of Electorals* and erased
                    from the Registry of Property,
if the ones who fertilize the coffee and sugar plantations
with their sweat,
if the ones who cut down the heavy forests with their machete blows
to increase the worldwide production of pineapple,
if all of them and their many other
malnourished
brothers,

---

* The reference to the Center of Electorals is to fraud in Mexican politics, which has been common in the
modern era.

sufriesen en su carne
la quemadura de la nefanda escoria
de la dignidad,
acaso
pretendiesen ser libres.
                    Y entonces
¿qué sería de las grandes Compañías,
de los *trusts* y los *cartels,*
de los jugadores de Bolsa
y de los propietarios de prostíbulos?

En nombre de esos valores fundamentales
y de otros menos cotizados,
alguien debe hacer algo
para evitarlo.

Pero
ha estallado una perla.
Peligroso es ahora el viento del Caribe.
Entre el olor salobre de la mar,
y el aroma más denso de las frutas del Trópico,
entre el brillante polen de las flores
que crecen donde el sol es un flagelo
infatigable y amarillo,
entre plumas de verdes papagallos,
y golpes de guitarras, y sonrisas
blancas como canciones en la noche,
el viento arrastra una semilla
perfumada y violenta,
una simiente fina como el polvo,
nube dorada o resplandor sin nube,
que los tifones lanzan—trizada
perla—contra las costas más lejanas,
y las brisas recogen y pasean,
y las lluvias abaten—astillada
Antilla—sobre el suelo,

suffer the scald
of their flesh on the vile slag-heap
of dignity,
perhaps
they would endeavor to be free.

And then
what will become of the great Companies,
of the trusts and cartels,
of the gamblers in the Stock Market
and the proprietors of brothels?

In the name of these fundamental values
and others less valuable,
someone should do something
to avoid it.

But
a pearl has exploded.
Now the Caribbean wind is dangerous.
Between the salty odor of the ocean waves,
and the dense aroma of the fruits of the Tropics,
among the brilliant pollen of the flowers
that grow where the sun is a yellow
and relentless whip,
among the green plumage of parrots,
and the strum of guitars, and white
smiles like songs in the night,
the wind carries a perfumed
and violent seed,
a seed fine like dust,
golden cloud or radiance without cloud,
that the typhoons hurl—shattered
pearl—against the farthest coasts,
and the breezes pick up and scatter,
and the rains dismantle—splintered
Antilles—upon the ground,

tormenta ciega o cielo derribado
—izada Cuba, como una bandera—
llama implacable o luz definidora,
mas siempre pura, viva, poderosa,
fértil semilla de la libertad.

blind storm or sky knocked down
—Cuba hoisted like a flag—
implacable flame or defining light,
but always pure, alive, powerful,
fertile seed of freedom.

CAMPOSANTO EN COLLIURE

Aquí paz
y después gloria.

Aquí
a orillas de Francia
en donde Cataluña no muere todavía
y prolonga en carteles de "Toros á Ceret"
y de "Flamenco's Show"
esa curiosa España de las ganaderías
de reses bravas y de juergas sórdidas,
reposa un español bajo una losa:
                                        paz
y después gloria.

Dramático destino,
triste suerte
morir aquí
            —paz
y después . . . —
                        perdido,
abandonado
y liberado a un tiempo
(ya sin tiempo)
de una patria sombría e inclemente.

Sí; después gloria.

Al final del verano,
por las proximidades
pasan trenes nocturnos, subrepticios,

CEMETERY IN COLLIURE

Here peace,
and later glory.

Here,
on the border of France,
where Catalonia does not yet die
and lives on in posters of "Toros á Ceret"
and "Flamenco's Show"
that curious Spain of cattle ranches,
fighting bulls and sordid revelry,
rests a Spaniard under a grave marker:

                                    peace,
and later glory.

Dramatic destiny,
sad misfortune
to die here
            —peace
and later . . . —
                        lost,
abandoned
and liberated to a time
(already timeless)
of a somber and inclement motherland.

Yes; later glory.

Through the nearby countryside,
at the end of summer,
nocturnal trains pass, surreptitious,

Note: Colliure, on the border of Spain and France, is where Antonio Machado died while fleeing Franco's
forces and was buried.

rebosantes de humana mercancía:
mano de obra barata, ejército
vencido por el hambre
                    —paz . . . —,
otra vez desbandada de españoles
cruzando la frontera, derrotados
— . . . sin gloria.

Se paga con la muerte
o con la vida,
pero se paga siempre una derrota.

¿Qué precio es el peor?
                    Me lo pregunto
y no sé qué pensar
ante esta tumba,
ante esta paz
                    —"Casino
de Canet: spanish gypsy dancers",
rumor de trenes, hojas . . . —,
ante la gloria ésta
— . . . de reseco laurel—
que yace aquí, abatida
bajo el ciprés erguido,
igual que una bandera al pie de un mástil.

Quisiera,
a veces,
que borrase el tiempo
los nombres y los hechos de esta historia
como borrará un día mis palabras
que la repiten siempre tercas, roncas.

overflowing with human cargo;
cheap laborers, an army
conquered by hunger
                              —peace . . . —,
Spaniards, once again fleeing in disarray,
crossing the frontier, defeated
— . . . without glory.

Whether in death
or life,
in defeat there's always a price to pay.

Which is worse?
                    I ask myself,
standing before this grave,
before this peace,
and don't know what to think
                                        "Casino
de Canet: spanish gypsy dancers,"
rumors of trains, leaves . . . —,
before this glory
— . . . of dried laurel—
lying here, knocked down
beneath the erect cypress,
just like the flag at the foot of a mast.

I wish,
sometimes,
that time would erase
the names and facts of this history
just as it will one day erase my words
that I will always repeat stubbornly, hoarsely.

ELEGIDO POR ACLAMACIÓN

Sí, fue un malentendido.
                            Gritaron: ¡a las urnas!
y él entendió: ¡a las armas!—dijo luego.
Era pundonoroso y mató mucho.
Con pistolas, con rifles, con decretos.

Cuando envainó la espada dijo, dice:
La democracia es lo perfecto.
El público aplaudió. Sólo callaron,
impasibles, los muertos.

El deseo popular será cumplido.
A partir de esta hora soy—silencio—
el Jefe, si queréis. Los disconformes
que levanten el dedo.

Inmóvil mayoría de cadáveres
le dio el mando total del cementerio.

ELECTED BY ACCLAMATION

Yes, it was a misunderstanding.
                                        They yelled: *Vote!*
And he heard: *Shoot!*—he said later.
He was honorable and killed thousands.
With guns, rifles, and decrees.

When he sheathed his sword, he said:
Democracy is best.
The crowds applauded. Only the impassive
dead bodies didn't say anything.

The popular will shall be accomplished.
Since I am now—silence—
if you wish, Commander-in-Chief. Raise your hand
if you disagree.

The motionless majority of the corpses
gave him total command of the cemetery.

Note: This poem refers to Francisco Franco, dictator of Spain (1939–75).

LECCIÓN DE LITERATURA

A Antonio Machado

La España de charanga y pandereta
devota de Frascuelo y de María,
ha de tener su marmol y su día.
—Antonio Machado

Los olmos sobreviven.
Las colinas
continúan dorándose
cuando el trigo madura, en primavera.
Los vencejos
regresan cada año, y las cigüeñas
reconquistan sus nidos
en febrero y en torres eclesiásticas
o álamos ribereños.
La tierra
se obstina en ser hermosa:
fina, adusta, guerrera.
Pese a tu muerte
—y a la de otros muchos—
también los hombres son como eran antes.
Devociones no idénticas
—Frascuelo es sólo un nombre—,
pero muy parecidas
están vigentes hoy igual que antaño:
Di Stéfano y la Misma
acaparan plegarias y ovaciones.
Todo ocurrió tal como nos dijiste:
del vano vientre del ayer surgieron

THE LESSON OF LITERATURE

To Antonio Machado

> That Spain of brass bands and tambourines,
> devoted to Frascuelo and the Virgin Mary,
> must have its marble and its day.
> —Antonio Machado

The elms survive.
The hills
continue to turn gold
as the wheat matures, in spring.
The swifts
return each year, and the storks,
in February, retake
their nests in the church steeples
or the poplars by the river.
The earth
persists in being beautiful:
delicate, austere, warlike.
In spite of your death
—and of so many others—
mankind also remains the same.
Devotions not identical
—Frascuelo is only a name—,
but very similar,
as valid today as in the past:
Di Stefano and the Lady
monopolize ovations and prayers.
Everything happened just as you told us it would:
these empty days emerged

Note: Frascuelo was a Spanish bullfighter during the late 1800s. DiStefano was a famous soccer star in Spain, although originally from Argentina, during the 1950s.

estos días vacios
y, orando y embistiendo,
calvas y calaveras venerables
nos predican traición y tradiciones.
Tú sigues siendo Don Antonio, siempre,
poeta vivo entre nosotros—muertos—
y te leemos cada día porque
nunca nos engañaste
y desenmarañaste el negro ovillo
de nuestra amarga historia
con dedos claros, delicados, duros.
Predejiste los tiempos que cruzamos
y los que cualquier día alcanzaremos.
La España de la rabia y de la idea
avanza, pese a todo. Te escuchamos:

Mas otra España nace . . .

                              Y te creemos.

from yesterday's vain belly
and, praying and charging,
bald and venerable skulls
preach treason and tradition.
You are still Don Antonio, always,
a poet alive among us—the dead—
and we read you each day because
you never deceived us
and you disentangled the black skein
of our bitter history
with clear, delicate, hard fingers.
You predicted the times we would go through
and those we will one day come to.
Despite everything, the Spain
of fury and thought advances. We hear you:

Another Spain is being born . . .

And we believe you.

PALABRA SOBRE PALABRA

1965

WORD UPON WORD

1965

LA PALABRA

Hace miles de años,
alguien,
un esclavo quizá,
descansando a la sombra de los árboles,
furtivamente,
en un lugar aislado
del fértil territorio
conquistado por su dueño el guerrero,
al contemplar los campos
regados por el río
  —probablemente
no ocurrió nada así:
reconstruyo, sin datos, una escena
que nadie sabe cómo ha sucedido—
y ver cómo otros hombres
cuidaban de las viñas, podaban
los olivos, transportaban el agua
que habría de mojar la tierra donde
crecían las hortalizas,
o conducían rebaños hacia el monte,
o extraían la miel de las colmenas

—me parece escuchar el rumor duro
del estío,
las metálicas hojas de los árboles
(perdida su humedad) crujiendo casi
al ser rozadas por el seco viento,
el batir firme y alto de las alas
de un águila, la viva luz
aplastándolo todo con su peso—,

y fijándose acaso especialmente
en el volumen firme e insinuado
bajo el gastado lino

THE WORD

Thousands of years ago,
someone,
a slave perhaps,
furtively
rested in the shade of trees
in a place isolated
from the fertile land
conquered by his master, the warrior,
and contemplated the fields
irrigated by a river
           —probably
nothing really happened like this:
I try to piece together, without facts,
what no one really knows—
and seeing how other men
took care of their vineyards, pruning
the olive trees, carrying water
to irrigate land
to grow vegetables,
or taking flocks to the mountains,
or honey from the beehives

—It seems to me I hear the harsh rumor of
summer:
the metallic leaves of the trees
(having lost their humidity) almost crackling
when caressed by the dry wind,
the firm wing beat
of an eagle high above, the vivid light
flattening everything with its weight—,

and perhaps showing special interest
in the firm and insinuated bulk
beneath the worn cloth

del vientre grávido de una mujer muy joven,
cerró un momento los cansados ojos
(el hombre que miraba todo aquello)
y articuló un suspiro
o bien dijo un sollozo,
o algo semejante
que repitió, y creció, y dejó su pecho
estremecido—así la rama
abandonada por un pájaro . . .

Igual que un pájaro
salta desde una rama,
de ese modo
surgió en el aire limpio de aquel día
la palabra:
> *amor.*
>   Era
suficiente.

Pronunciada primero,
luego escrita,
la palabra pasó de boca en boca,
siguió de mano en mano,
de cera en pergamino,
de papel en papel,
de tinta en tinta,
fue tallada en madera,
cayó sobre las láminas
olorosas y blancas,
y llegó hasta nosotros
impresa y negra, viva
tras un largo pasaje por los siglos
llamados de oro,
por las gloriosas épocas,

of the pregnant belly of a very young woman,
and closing his tired eyes for a moment
(the man seeing all of this)
and sighed,
or perhaps he sobbed,
or uttered something similar
he repeated, and it grew, and left his chest
shaking—just like a branch
when abandoned by a bird . . .

Just like a bird
springs from its branch,
in this way
the word emerged into the clean air
of that day:
    love.
      It was
enough.

First pronounced,
later written,
the word passed from mouth to mouth,
then from hand to hand,
from wax on parchment,
from paper to paper,
from ink to ink,
it was carved in wood,
fell upon the scented
and white laminations,
and then came to us
printed and black, alive
after its long journey through the so-called
"golden ages,"
through the glorious epochs,

a través de los textos conocidos
con el nombre de clásicos más tarde.

Retrotraerse a un sentimiento puro,
imaginar un mundo en sus pre-nombres,
es imposible ahora.

La palabra fue dicha para siempre.
Para todos, también.
                        Yo la recojo,
la elijo entre otras muchas,
la empaño con mi aliento
y la lanzo,
pájaro o piedra,
de nuevo al aire,
                al sol,
                        hoy

                                (rostros, árboles,
nubes: todo es distinto en esta
primavera. En el vaso,
el agua huele a río.
Como una larga cabellera, el viento
ondea por las calles y se abate
de pronto
rizado y frío sobre el suelo.
Y en ocasiones,
¿por qué mi pensanmiento
no acompaña a mis ojos,
y se aleja
de lo que ven, perdido
y a la vez fijo en algo . . . ?),
                        porque quiero.

through the texts that much later
came to be known as "the classics."

It's impossible now
to recapture a pure sentiment,
to imagine a world before it's named.

The word has been spoken for eternity.
For everyone.
                    I pick it up,
I choose it from among many others,
I moisten it with my breath
and throw it once again,
bird or stone,
new into the air,
                    to the sun,
                              today
                                   (faces, trees,
clouds—everything is different this
spring In the glass
the water smells of river.
Like a long head of hair, the wind
weaves through the streets and
all of a sudden,
curled and cold, falls to the ground.
And on occasion,
why do my thoughts
not follow my eyes,
and drift away
from what they see, lost
and at the same time fixed on something . . . ?),
                              because it's what I desire.

En ocasiones,
el corazón se siente abrumado por la melancolía,
y al pensamiento llegan
viejas palabras leídas en libros olvidados:
felicidad, misterio, alma, infinito.

¿Es la tarde que mete sus uñas venenosas
en el sombrío cuerpo del olvido
y huye hacia la noche llevándose en la boca
algún gesto borroso,
una canción perdida,
la desteñida cinta que no pudo
atar tantos recuerdos?

Pero no.
            En esta hora, la nostalgia
no viene del ayer,
sino del ahora mismo,
del solohaceuninstante que estabas a mi lado,
rasgando
con tus dientes de niña
la penumbra,
rompiendo la raíz de mi tristeza
y alzando en su lugar un árbol de alegría,

La claridad evanescente, como
un animal incierto,
salta—quizá en busca de ti—
por la ventana de la alcoba
donde mi rostro abandonado intenta
penetrar en lo oscuro:
nada tras de la sombra, sino sombras.
Tras de ti misma,
tu ausencia se dibuja

WORDS ALMOST FORGOTTEN

On occasion,
the heart feels overwhelmed by melancholy,
and I think of
old words read in forgotten books:
happiness, mystery, soul, infinity.

Is it the evening that thrusts its poisoned fingernail
into the somber body of forgetfulness
and runs away into the night carrying in its mouth
some blurry gesture,
a lost song,
the faded ribbon that could not
tie up so many memories?

But no.
       In this hour, nostalgia
doesn't come from yesterday,
but from right now
from just a moment ago
when you were at my side
tearing the penumbra
with your childlike teeth,
breaking the root of my sadness
and raising in its place a tree of happiness.

An evanescent clarity, like
an uncertain animal,
jumps—perhaps in search of you—
through the window of my bedroom
where my abandoned countenance tries
to penetrate the darkness:
nothing behind the shadow except shadows.
Behind you,
like a terrifying nothingness,

como una nada pavorosa:
                              el tiempo
que debo estar sin ti
es la aguda herramienta que el destino utiliza
para cerrarme el paso a la esperanza.

Añorar el futuro que no existe
es aceptar la vida despojada
de sus días mejores,
y vivir es igual que haber vivido
ya, sin que ese haber vivido
suponga—por desgracia—estar ya muerto.

De esa forma,
porvenir y pasado se confunden
y el tiempo no sucede,
y uno existe
sin recuerdos ni afanes,
igual que un dios pequeño y miserable
que no tiene memoria
porque todo para él está presente:
como
esas viejas palabras
                    —*felicidad, misterio* . . . —
que hoy vuelven a mis manos
—¿desde cuándo?—
y que ahora escribo
                    — . . . *alma* . . . —,
                                    sin vergüenza,
para ti, porque tuyo
es todo lo que pienso
                    — . . . *infinito*—
y lo será por siempre
hasta los límites donde mi fe alcanza.

your absence materializes:
                              the time
that I must be without you
is the sharp tool that destiny utilizes
to block my path to hope.

To long for a future that no longer exists
is to accept that life is stripped
of its best days,
and to live is equal to having lived
already, but having lived
doesn't imply—unfortunately—being already dead.

In this way,
future and past are confused,
and time doesn't happen,
and one exists
without memories or desires,
just like a small and miserable god
who has no memory
because everything for him is the present:
like
those old words
                    —*happiness, mystery . . .* —
that return today to my hands
—since when?—
and that I now write
                    — *. . . soul . . .* —,
                                        without shame,
for you, because yours
is everything that I think of
                    — *. . . infinity*—
and it will be for always
until my faith reaches its limits.

ME BASTA ASÍ

Si yo fuese Dios
y tuviese el secreto,
haría
un ser exacto a ti;
lo probaría
(a la manera de los panaderos
cuando prueban el pan, es decir:
con la boca),
y si ese sabor fuese
igual al tuyo, o sea
tu mismo olor, y tu manera
de sonreír,
y de guardar silencio,
y de estrechar mi mano estrictamente,
y de besarnos sin hacernos daño
—de esto sí estoy seguro: pongo
tanta atención cuando te beso—;
                       entonces,
si yo fuese Dios,
podría repetirte y repetirte,
siempre la misma y siempre diferente,
sin cansarme jamás del juego idéntico,
sin desdeñar tampoco la que fuiste
por la que ibas a ser dentro de nada;
ya no sé si me explico, pero quiero
aclarar que si yo fuese
Dios, haría
lo posible por ser Ángel González
para quererte tal como te quiero,
para aguardar con calma
a que te crees tú misma cada día,
a que sorprendas todas las mañanas
la luz recién nacida con tu propia
luz, y corras

THAT'S ENOUGH FOR ME

If I were God
and knew the secret,
I would make
someone just like you;
and I would test my creation
(the way they say
bakers do when they taste bread:
with their mouths),
and if that taste were
the same as yours, I mean,
your same smell, and your way
of smiling,
and of being silent,
and holding my hand tightly,
and just like the way we kiss each other without hurting
—and I'm sure of that: I'm
so careful when I kiss you—
                    then,
if I were God,
I could duplicate you over and over,
always the same and yet different,
without ever getting tired of the game,
or without scorning the one you were
for the one you will be in the next moment;
I'm not sure I'm making myself clear, but I want
to explain that if I were
God, I would do everything
possible to be Ángel González,
to love you just as I love you now,
to wait calmly
until you recreate yourself each day,
until each morning you surprise
the newborn light with your own
light, and draw

la cortina impalpable que separa
el sueño de la vida,
resucitándome con tu palabra,
Lázaro alegre,
yo,
mojado todavía
de sombras y pereza,
sorprendido y absorto
en la contemplación de todo aquello
que, en unión de mí mismo,
recuperas y salvas, mueves, dejas
abandonado cuando—luego—callas . . .
(Escucho tu silencio.
                            Oigo
constelaciones: existes.
                        Creo en ti.
                                Eres.
                                Me basta.)

the imperceptible curtain that separates
life from dream,
bringing me to life with your word,
happy Lazarus,
I,
still damp
with shadows and laziness,
surprised and absorbed
in the contemplation of everything
that, in union with myself,
you recover and save, you move, you leave
abandoned when—later—you remain silent . . .
(I listen to your silence.

                   I hear
constellations: you exist.
                I believe in you.
                      You are.
                        That's enough for me.)

Aborrezco este oficio algunas veces:
espía de palabras, busco,
busco
el término huidizo,
la expresión inestable
que signifique, exacta, lo que eres.

Inmóvil en la nada, al margen
de la vida (hundido
en un denso silencio sólo roto
por el batir oscuro de mi sangre),
busco,
busco aquellas palabras
que no existen
—quizá sirvan: *delicia de tu cuello* . . . —
que te acosan y mueren sin rozarte,
cuando lo que quisiera
es llegar a tu cuello
con mi boca
— . . . o acaso: *increíble sonrisa que he besado*—,
subir hasta tu boca
con mis labios,
sujetar con mis manos tu cabeza
y ver
allá en el fondo de tus ojos,
instantes antes de cerrar los míos,
paz verde y luz dormida,
claras sombras
          —tal vez
fuera mejor decir: *humo en la tarde,*
borrosa música que llueve del otoño,
niebla que cae despacio sobre un valle—
avanzando hacia mí,
girando,

USELESS WORDS

There are times when I hate this profession,
a word spy, I hunt,
hunt for
the furtive word,
the uneasy expression
that means exactly what you are.

Motionless in the void, at the edge
of life (sinking
into a dense silence broken only
by the dark heart beat of my blood),
I hunt,
hunt for those words
that don't exist
—perhaps these will do: *the delight of your throat . . .* —
and pursue you and die without touching you,
when what I would like
is to touch your throat
with my mouth
— . . . or perhaps: *unbelievable smile that I've kissed*—,
or go up to your mouth
with my lips,
hold your head between my hands
and gaze
down into the depths of your eyes,
an instant before I close my eyes,
at the green peace and sleeping light,
bright shadows
                 —perhaps
it would be better to say: *evening smoke,*
faint music that the autumn rains down,
fog that falls slowly upon a valley—
advancing toward me,
spinning,

penetrándome
hasta anegar mi pecho y levantar
mi corazón salvado, ileso, en vilo
sobre la leve espuma de la dicha.

penetrating me
until it floods my chest and lifts
my redeemed heart, unharmed, suspended
above the faint foam of happiness.

TRATADO DE URBANISMO

1967

TREATISE ON URBAN DEVELOPMENT

1967

Son pocos.
La primavera está muy prestigiada, pero
es mejor el verano.
Y también esas grietas que el otoño
forma al interceder con los domingos
en algunas ciudades
ya de por sí amarillas como plátanos.
El invierno elimina muchos sitios:
quicios de puertas orientadas al norte,
orillas de los ríos,
bancos públicos.
Los contrafuertes exteriores
de las viejas iglesias
dejan a veces huecos
utilizables aunque caiga nieve.
Pero desengañémonos: las bajas
temperaturas y los vientos húmedos
lo dificultan todo.
Las ordenanzas, además, proscriben
la caricia (con exenciones
para determinadas zonas epidérmicas
—sin interés alguno—
en niños, perros y otros animales)
y el "no tocar, peligro de ignominia"
puede leerse en miles de miradas.
¿A dónde huir, entonces?
Por todas partes ojos bizcos,
córneas torturadas,
implacables pupilas,
retinas reticentes,
vigilan, desconfían, amenazan.
Queda quizá el recurso de andar solo,
de vaciar el alma de ternura
y llenarla de hastío e indiferencia,
en este tiempo hostil, propicio al odio.

There aren't many.
Spring is highly esteemed, but
summer is better.
And also those crevices that autumn makes
when it intercedes with Sundays
in some cities
that are already as yellow as bananas.
Winter eliminates many places:
doorways facing north,
riverbanks,
public benches.
Buttresses outside
old churches
sometimes leave usable
hollows even if snow is falling.
But let's not fool ourselves: cold
temperatures and damp winds
make everything difficult.
Besides, regulations forbid
fondling (except for
predetermined areas of the skin
—of no interest at all—
of children, dogs, and other animals)
and *do not touch under peril of disgrace*
can be read in thousands of glances.
To where does one escape, then?
Everywhere squinting eyes,
tortured corneas,
implacable pupils,
reticent retinas,
are vigilant, suspicious, threatening.
Perhaps one has the option of going it alone,
of emptying the soul of tenderness
and filling it with boredom and indifference,
in this hostile time, propitious for hatred.

. . . y las muchachas andan con las piernas desnudas:
¿por qué las utilizan
para andar?
Mentalmente repaso
oficios convincentes
para ellas—las piernas—,
digamos: situaciones
más útiles al hombre
que las mira
despacio,
silbando entre los dientes
una canción recuperada
apenas
   —ese oficio no me gusta . . . —
en el acantilado del olvido.
Si bien se mira, bien se ve que todas
son bellas: las que pasan
llevando hacia otro sitio
cabellos, voces, senos,
ojos, gestos, sonrisas;
las que permanecen
cruzadas,
dobladas como ramas bajo el peso
de la belleza cálida, caída
desde el dulce abandono de los cuerpos sentados;
las esbeltas y largas;
las tersas y bruñidas; las cubiertas
de leve vello, tocadas por la gracia
de la luz, color miel, comestibles
y apetitosas como frutas frescas;
y también—sobre todo—aquellas que demoran
su pesado trayecto hasta el tobillo
en el curvo perfil que delimita
las pueriles, alegres, inocentes,

PUBLIC GARDEN WITH PARTICULAR LEGS

. . . and the young women walk by with bare legs:
why do they use them
to walk?
Thinking over
useful tasks
for them—the legs—,
we could say: there are more
useful situations for the man
who looks so slowly
at them,
whistling between his teeth
a scarcely recoverable
song
       —this job doesn't please me . . . —
in the cliffs of forgetfulness.
If you look closely, you can see that
they are all beautiful: the ones that pass
carrying toward other places
hair, voices, breasts,
eyes, gestures, smiles;
the ones that remain
cross-legged
bent like branches under the weight
of the warmest beauty, fallen
from the sweet abandonment of the seated bodies;
the slender and long;
the smooth and tanned; the ones
with slight down, touched by the gift
of light, honey-colored, edible
and as tempting to the taste as fresh fruit;
and also—above all—those that delay
their heavy fall toward the ankle
in the curved profile that limits
the puerile, happy, innocent,

irreflexivas, blancas pantorrillas.
Pensándolo mejor, duele mirarlas:
tanta gracia dispersa, inaccesible,
abandonada entre la primavera,
abruma el corazón del conmovido
espectador
que siente la humillante quemadura
de la renuncia,
y maldice en voz baja,
y se apoya en la verja del estanque,
y mira el agua,
y ve su propio rostro,
y escupe distraído, mientras sigue
con los ojos los círculos
que trazan en la tensa superficie
su soledad, su miedo, su saliva.

irreflexive, white calves.
Thinking it over, it's painful to look at them:
so much dispersed grace, inaccessible,
abandoned in the springtime,
oppressing the heart of the uncomfortable
observer,
who feels the humiliating burn
of resignation,
and curses in a whisper,
and leans over the grate of the pond,
and looks at the water
and sees his own face,
and spits distractedly, while following
with his eyes the circles
that trace in the tense surface
his saliva, his fear, his solitude.

LOS SÁBADOS, LAS PROSTITUTAS MADRUGAN MUCHO PARA ESTAS DISPUESTAS

Elena despertó a las dos y cinco,
abrió despacio las contraventanas
y el sol de invierno hirió sus ojos
enrojecidos. Apoyada
la frente en el cristal,
miró a la calle: niños con bufandas,
perros. Tres curas
paseaban.
En ese mismo instante,
Dora comenzaba
a ponerse las medias.
Las ligas le dejaban
una marca en los muslos ateridos.
Al encender la radio—"Aída:
marcha triunfal"—,
recordaba palabras
—"Dora, Dorita, te amo"—
a la vez que intentaba
reconstruir el rostro de aquel hombre
que se fue ayer—es decir, hoy—de madrugada,
y leía distraída una moneda:
"Veinticinco pesetas." " . . . por la gracia
de Dios."
                    (Y por la cama)
Eran las tres y diez cuando Conchita
se estiraba
la piel de las mejillas
frente al espejo. Bostezó. Miraba
su propio rostro con indiferencia.
Localizó tres canas
en la raíz oscura de su pelo
amarillo. Abrió luego una caja
de crema rosa, cuyo contenido

ON SATURDAYS, THE PROSTITUTES GET UP VERY EARLY
TO GET READY

Elena woke up at five after two,
and slowly opened the shutters
to a winter sun that stung her
reddened eyes. Resting her forehead
on the windowpane,
she looked out at the street: children wearing scarves,
dogs. Three priests
walked by.
At this same instant
Dora began
to put on her stockings.
The garters left
a mark on her numb thighs.
Turning on the radio—"Aida:
The Wedding March"—
she recalled the words
—"Dora, Dorita, I love you"—
at the same time she tried
to remember the face of the man
who left yesterday—or rather, today—at dawn,
and distracted, read the inscription on a coin:
"Twenty-five pesetas." " . . . by the grace
of God."
        (And by the grace of the bed.)
It was ten after three when Conchita
stretched
the skin of her cheeks
in front of the mirror. She yawned. She looked
indifferently at her face.
She found three gray hairs
in the dark roots of her bleached
hair. Then she opened a jar
of pink cream, which she

extendió en torno a su nariz. Bostezaba,
y aprovechó aquel gesto
indefinible para
comprobar el estado
de una muela cariada
allá en el fondo de sus fauces secas,
inofensivas, turbias, algo hepáticas.
Por otra parte,
también se preparaba
la ciudad.
El tren de las catorce treinta y nueve
alteró el ritmo de las calles. Miradas
vacilantes, ojos
confusos, planteaban
imprecisas preguntas
que las bocas no osaban
formular.
En los cafés, entraban
y salían los hombres, movidos
por algo parecido a una esperanza.
Se decía que aún era temprano. Pero
a las cuatro, Dora comenzaba
a quitarse las medias—las ligas
dejaban una marca
en sus muslos.
Lentas, solemnes, eclesiásticas,
volaban de las torres
palomas y campanas.
Mientras
se bajaba la falda,
Conchita vio su cuerpo
—y otra sombra vaga—
moverse en el espejo
de su alcoba. En las calles y plazas
palidecía la tarde de diciembre. Elena
cerró despacio las contraventanas.

applied to her nose. Yawning,
she took advantage of that indefinable
gesture to
check the condition
of a decayed tooth
at the back of her dried-up, inoffensive,
stained, slightly jaundiced jaws.
At the same time
the city was getting
ready.
The two thirty-nine train
changed the rhythm of the streets. Vacillating
glances, confused
eyes, raised
vague questions
that mouths didn't dare
ask.
In the cafés, men
entered and left, moved
by something similar to hope.
It could be said that it was still early. But
at four o'clock, Dora began
to take off her stockings—her garters
left a mark
on her thighs.
Slow, solemn, ecclesiastical,
pigeons and bells
sprang from the towers.
Taking off
her skirt
Conchita saw her body
—and another vague shadow—
move in her bedroom
mirror. In the streets and plazas,
the December afternoon faded. Elena
slowly closed the shutters.

ZONA RESIDENCIAL

Hasta un ciego podría adivinarlo:
la perfección reside en estas calles.

Los ruidos, los olores,
el timbre delicado
de las voces humanas, el júbilo
de los ladridos,
el rumor armonioso de los coches,
la discreta presencia de las lilas,
incluso
la templanza del aire que difunde su aroma,
revelan, sin más datos,
eso que la mirada
comprueba

       en las palomas viandantes

(remisas a la hora
de abandonar las migas
de pan, pese a la terca
irrupción de pisadas o neumáticos),

en la actitud cortés de los jardines
particulares

       (generosos no sólo
en la distribución de polen y fragancia,
sino también volcados en la entrega
del cuerpo mismo de las flores
que se ofrecen, abiertas y sumisas,
entre las verjas y sobre las tapias),

en las personas y sus atributos:

RESIDENTIAL ZONE

Even a blind man could see it:
perfection resides in these streets.

The sounds, odors,
the delicate timbre
of human voices, the jubilation
of barking dogs,
the harmonious murmur of cars,
the discrete presence of lilies,
indeed
the mildness of the air that diffuses their aroma,
reveals, without any other information,
that which the gaze
confirms

        in the passing doves

(slow to
abandon crumbs
of bread, regardless of obstinate
interruptions from footsteps or cars),

in the courteous attitude of private
gardens

        (not only generous
in the distribution of pollen and fragrance,
but also abandoned in their surrender,
the same flowers
that offer themselves, open and submissive,
between the fence and upon the garden wall),

in the people and their attributes:

niños
(bicicletas y risas niqueladas),

militares
(de alta graduación, sin sable
ni escopeta, sólo
con artritismo y condecoraciones),

adolescentes
(de agradable formato, encuadernados
en piel de calidad insuperable)

doncellas
(del servicio doméstico
—se entiende—,
también bellas debajo de la cofia),

y otros seres adultos
(señoras de buen porte, caballeros
de excelentes modales,
carteros presurosos,
conductores corteses) . . .

Todo, en resumen, lo que ven los ojos
o escuchan, tocan, huelen los sentidos,
es síntoma, sin duda,
de la bondad, del orden, de la dicha
que ha de albergar un mundo tan perfecto.

children
(bicycles and chromium-plated laughter),

the military
(discharged at retirement, without swords
or rifles, just
arthritis and insignia),

adolescents
(of pleasant demeanor, bound
in skins of insuperable quality)

maids
(of domestic service
—it's understood—
also beautiful beneath their hair nets),

and others
(ladies of good carriage, gentlemen
with excellent manners,
speedy postmen,
courteous conductors) . . .

Everything, in summary, that the eyes see
or hear, or touch, that the senses smell,
is symptom, no doubt,
of humility, of order, of the happiness
that harbors a world so perfect.

PARQUE PARA DIFUNTOS

En el jardín germinan los cadáveres.
La pompa de la rosa
jamás, no, nunca es fúnebre.
Únicamente, al entreabrir sus pétalos
devuelve una de tantas
sonrisas que no, nunca, jamás se produjeron
y que la tierra se tragó nonatas.
                                    Lo mismo
podríamos afirmar de las magnolias
respecto
al impreciso nácar de esas ingles
jamás, nunca, no vistas hasta ahora
con una opacidad tan delicada,
luminosa y sombría al mismo tiempo

(Pienso:
            cuando tú hayas muerto,
¿qué flor será capaz de recoger
aunque tan sólo sea
una mínima parte
del perfil delicado de tu cuello?;
jamás, ninguna, nunca,
                            —pienso.)

La brisa,
al conmover las ramas del cerezo,
dispersa
una eyaculación de leves hojas blancas
sobre los ojerosos pensamientos:
así retorna al aire un afán enterrado,
vuelve a latir, regresa
un perdido deseo.

Hay margaritas entre el césped—¡cuántas!

PARK FOR THE DEAD

In the garden the cadavers germinate.
The pomp of the rose
is never, no, never funeral.
Only, as its petals open
does it return one of many
smiles that never, no, never became
and that the earth swallowed unborn.

                                The same
could be said of the magnolias
regarding
the imprecise pearlness of these groins
never, no, never seen until now
with an opacity so delicate,
luminous and somber at the same time.

(I think:
          when you die,
which flower will dare to pick up
even a minimal part
of the delicate profile of your neck?;
never, none, never,
                —I think.)

The breeze,
as it shakes the branches of the cherry tree,
disperses
an ejaculation of light, white leaves
over the seedy thoughts:
so a buried anxiety returns to the air,
it beats again, returns
a lost wish.

There are daisies in the grass—So many!
Wan transients, they circulate

Circulan transeúntes macilentos
por los senderos soleados. Rezan
—*luego existimos,* creen. Pasan
sin escuchar el grito luminoso
de los lirios,
sin advertir el gesto
de las dalias doradas, que señalan
sus lúgubres figuras con sus múltiples dedos.

Pronto lo veréis todo a través de mi tallo
—susurra un nomeolvides—,
periscopio final de vuestros sueños.

through the sunlit paths. They pray
—*then we exist,* they believe. They pass
without hearing the luminous shouts
of the iris,
not noticing the gesture
of the golden dahlias, that point to
their mournful figures with their multiple fingers.

Soon you will see it all through my stem
—whispers one forget-me-not—,
final periscope of your dreams.

CENTRO COMERCIAL

Si una luz simboliza la esperanza,
múltiples luces ¿simbolizan
múltiples esperanzas? O acaso
la desesperación
    —para aquellos que creen
que sólo hay una necesaria . . .

El constelado suelo
enciende, apaga, enciende
rutilantes estrellas.
Las dinamos generan nebulosas
de inflamado neón,
asteroides bifásicos,
cometas con su ardiente cabellera
de bombillas fugaces
que cruzan, rayan, trazan
órbitas diminutas,
brillantes trayectorias,
señales de mercurio incandescente
en el turbio apogeo de la tarde.

Muchos son los llamados, mas no es fácil
interpretar los signos.
      El dedo
de la Publicidad,
con su crepuscular caligrafía,
aclara muchas cosas,
rotula los espacios, tiñe el aire,
delimita galaxias, difumina
polvo de kilovatios en las calles.

Abierto diariamente hasta las siete:
firmamento caído,
eternidad trizada a vuestro alcance.

THE MALL

If one light symbolizes hope,
multiple lights symbolize
multiple hopes? Or perhaps
hopelessness
               —for those that believe
there is only one necessary . . .

The constellated floor
turning on, turning off, turning on
shining stars.
Dynamos generating nebulas
of inflamed neon,
disphasic asteroids,
comets with their ardent hair
of escaping light bulbs
crossing, scratching, tracing
diminutive orbits,
brilliant trajectories,
signs of incandescent mercury
in the confused apogee of the evening.

Many are the called, but it's not easy
to interpret the signs.
                    The finger
of Advertising,
with its crepuscular calligraphy,
clarifies many things,
letters spaces, dyes the air,
defines galaxies, blurs
the dust of kilowatts in the streets.

Open daily until seven:
fallen firmament,
broken pieces of eternity within your reach.

Particular mención merecen las vitrinas
donde se exhiben modas de señora.
Los sombreros de paja de Florencia,
levemente dorados, mas sin brillo,
entonan con el fuego de un pañuelo
diseñado en París,
sobre el que,
            esbelto,
rodeado por las piedras (como gotas
de sangre) de un collar
falso hasta el éxtasis,
                    se eleva
—incómodo, exquisito, indiferente—
un zapato,
un único zapato inconcebible:
abrumador ejemplo de belleza,
catedral entrevista sin distancia
cantando con su esbelta arquitectura
un mudo "gloria en las alturas" a la
mórbida, larga, afortunada y fuerte
pierna posible que de su horma surja.

Aunque por todas partes (no ahí sólo)
la gracia de un color, el acabado
perfecto de una forma, o simplemente
la noble calidad de la materia,
reclaman la atención de los viandantes,
gritan, cantan, golpean sus sentidos.

No menos dulces fueron las canciones
que tentaron a Ulises en el curso
de su desesperante singladura,
pero iba atado al palo de la nave,
y la marinería, ensordecida

The latest women's fashions in the
glass case deserve particular mention.
Straw hats from Florence,
dull but lightly golden,
harmonize with the fire of a scarf
designed in Paris,
over which,
        slender,
surrounded by the stones (like drops
of blood) of a necklace
fake to the point of ecstasy,
                a shoe
—uncomfortable, exquisite, indifferent—
rises,
a singularly unique and inconceivable shoe:
an overwhelming example of beauty,
the cathedral glimpsed without distance
singing with its slender architecture
a mute "glory to the heights" to the
delicate, long, fortunate and strong
potential leg that might sprout from its shoe tree.

Even though everywhere (not just there)
the charm of a color, the perfect
finish to a shape, or simply
the noble quality of the material,
clamors for the attention of the passers-by,
whose shouts, and singing, hammer the senses.

No less sweet were the songs
that tempted Ulysses during the course
of his desperate voyage,
but he was tied to the mast,
and his crew, artificially

de forma artificial,
al no poder oír mantuvo el rumbo.

Mas la cuestión no es ésa:
íncubos o sirenas, ángeles
derribados o en activo, todos
esos objetos manufacturados, tantas
mercaderías y brillantes bienes,
¿se acercan
desde la lejanía de un mundo diferente,
más profundo y mejor,
para mostrar su perfección de seres
colmados, plenos, casi eternos,
o vienen
a contemplar la vida a la intemperie,
la indefensión cercada a cielo abierto,
el apacible tránsito del hombre
a manera de grey
por su cañada?

Así las cosas,
así las mercancías:
indiferentes, ciegos símbolos
de la felicidad, seguros
al otro lado del cristal manchado
con el aliento y la avidez de ese
tropel informe y presuroso
que vacila, se para, mira y sigue
buscando nuevas grietas en el muro.

deaf,
not hearing, kept to the straight course.

But that's not really the issue:
incubus, or siren, fallen angels
or angels on active duty, all
these manufactured objects, so much merchandise
and brilliant wealth,
they approach
from the remoteness of a different world,
more profound and better able
to reveal the perfections of its inhabitants,
replete, full, almost eternal,
or do they come
to contemplate life unsheltered
defenseless under the wide open sky,
the gentle transit of man,
the manner of his congregation,
through its glen?

In this way things,
in this way merchandise:
indifferent, blind symbols
of happiness, safe
on the other side of the window dirtied
by the breath and greediness of this
informed and hasty rush hour
that flickers, stops, looks and continues
to search for new cracks in the wall.

Como un estanque sucio,
el tiempo
cubrió con su agua turbia las palabras,
los discursos, las frases
cargadas de propósitos sinceros.
Hubo más que palabras, ciertamente.
Pero ahora
sólo quedan los muros,
impasibles testigos de esa historia
y de otras muchas más,
también pasadas.
El sol
dora los contrafuertes exteriores,
purifica las piedras y los vidrios,
resbala por las cúpulas, resurge
debajo de los arcos. Está
vacía la plaza,
crepuscular y clara,
llena de un aire limpio
de voces y de gestos.

Y sin embargo,
cuánta voz gritaría si pudiese,
cuánta sangre
—menos odiosa que esta indiferencia—
mancharía de rojo las paredes.

Respirando aquí el aire de la tarde,
oyendo así el silencio,
y recordando,
la vida es—o parece—
más absurda e irreal, más insensata.
¿Quién lo diría, ayer? Sin duda, entonces,

PLAZA WITH TOWERS AND PALACES

Like a dirty pond,
time
with its muddy water covered the words,
the speeches, the phrases
filled with sincere propositions.
Surely, there was more than words.
But now
only the walls remain,
impassive witnesses of that history
and of so many others,
also past.
The sun
gilds the buttresses,
purifies the stones and glass,
slips through the cupolas, reappears
beneath the arches. The square
is empty,
twilit and clear,
filled with an air cleansed
of voices and gestures.

And yet,
how many voices would speak out if they could,
how much blood
—less hateful than this indifference—
would stain the walls red.

However, breathing the evening air,
listening to the silence,
and remembering
life is—or seems to be—
more absurd and unreal, more senseless.
Who would have said it yesterday? No doubt, then

muchos.
      Hoy ya nadie.
            Silencio:
un murmullo de hojas
pasa de árbol a árbol
empujado hacia el campo por el viento.

many would have.
                    Today, no one.
                              Silence:
a murmur of leaves
passes from tree to tree
pushed towards the field by the wind.

PREÁMBULO A UN SILENCIO

Porque se tiene conciencia de la inutilidad de tantas
        cosas
a veces uno se sienta tranquilamente a la sombra de
        un árbol—en verano—
y se calla.

(¿Dije tranquilamente?: falso, falso:
uno se sienta inquieto haciendo extraños gestos,
pisoteando las hojas abatidas
por la furia de un otoño sombrío,
destrozando con los dedos el cartón inocente de una
        caja de fósforos,
mordiendo injustamente las uñas de esos dedos,
escupiendo en los charcos invernales,
golpeando con el puño cerrado la piel rugosa de las
        casas que permanecen indiferentes al paso de la
        primavera,
una primavera urbana que asoma con timidez los flecos
        de sus cabellos verdes allá arriba,
detrás del zinc oscuro de los canalones,
levemente arraigada a la materia efímera de las tejas a
        punto de ser polvo.)

Eso es cierto, tan cierto
como que tengo un nombre con alas celestiales,
arcangélico nombre que a nada corresponde:
Ángel,
me dicen,
y yo me levanto
disciplinado y recto
con las alas mordidas
—quiero decir: las uñas—
y sonrío y me callo porque, en último extremo,
uno tiene conciencia
de la inutilidad de todas las palabras.

Because one is aware of the uselessness of so many
    things
sometimes one sits peacefully in the shade of
    a tree—in summer—
and is silent.

(Did I say peacefully?: false, false:
one sits restlessly making strange gestures,
trampling the leaves knocked down
by the fury of the somber autumn,
breaking with the fingers the innocent cardboard box
    of matches,
biting unjustly the nails of those fingers,
spitting into water puddles,
banging with a clenched fist the corrugated skin of
    houses that remain indifferent to the passing of
    spring,
an urban spring that timidly reveals the
    fringes of its green hair way up above,
behind the dark zinc of the gutters,
lightly attached to the ephemeral material of the tiles
    that are about to turn to dust.)

This is certain, as certain
as saying that I have a name with celestial wings,
an archangelic name that corresponds to nothing:
Ángel,
they call me,
and I get up
disciplined and erect
with bitten wings
—I mean: nails—
and smile and I'm quiet because, in the end,
one is aware
of the utter uselessness of all words.

Una revolución.
Luego una guerra.
En aquellos dos años—que eran
la quinta parte de toda mi vida—,
yo había experimentado sensaciones distintas.
Imaginé más tarde
lo que es la lucha en calidad de hombre.
Pero como tal niño,
la guerra, para mí, era tan sólo:
suspensión de las clases escolares,
Isabelita en bragas en el sótano,
cementerios de coches, pisos
abandonados, hambre indefinible,
sangre descubierta
en la tierra o las losas de la calle,
un terror que duraba
lo que el frágil rumor de los cristales
después de la explosión,
y el casi incomprensible
dolor de los adultos,
sus lágrimas, su miedo,
su ira sofocada,
que, por algún resquicio,
entraban en mi alma
para desvanecerse luego, pronto,
ante uno de los muchos
prodigios cotidianos: el hallazgo
de una bala aún caliente
el incendio
de un edificio próximo,
los restos de un saqueo
—papeles y retratos
en medio de la calle . . .

A revolution.
Then a war.
In those two years—that were
a fifth of my whole life—,
I had mixed feelings.
I imagined later,
as a grown man, what conflict is like.
But as that child,
the war, for me, was simply:
dismissal of classes at school,
Isabelita in panties in the cellar,
automobile graveyards, abandoned
apartments, an indefinable hunger,
blood discovered
on the ground or cobblestones of the street,
a terror that lasted
just as long as the fragile sound of the windowpanes
after the explosion,
and the nearly incomprehensible
sorrow of the grown-ups,
their tears, their fear,
their repressed rage
that entered my soul
through some crack,
to disappear later, quickly,
in the face of one of the many
daily miracles: the discovery
of a still warm bullet,
the burning
of a nearby building,
the remains of a looting
—papers and photographs
in the middle of the street . . .

Todo pasó,
todo es borroso ahora, todo
menos eso que apenas percibía
en aquel tiempo
y que, años más tarde,
resurgió en mi interior, ya para siempre:
este miedo difuso,
esta ira repentina,
estas imprevisibles
y verdaderas ganas de llorar.

Now it's all gone,
everything is blurred now, everything
except for what I scarcely noticed
at the time
and which, many years later,
surged up again inside me, to remain forever:
this pervading fear,
this sudden rage,
this unpredictable
and profound desire to weep.

EVOCACIÓN SEGUNDA

Recuerdo a los indianos
de mi infancia.
Eran buenas personas, nos decían.
Donaban fuentes públicas
y grupos escolares a los pueblos
de donde
el hambre
los había expulsado cuando niños
de su débil reducto nutritivo,
defendidos
de la tuberculosis
sólo por el maíz y las patatas.
Regalaban también brillantes cálices
de oro a las iglesias,
coronas refulgentes a las vírgenes
de madera, y valiosas monedas
a las vírgenes otras: las de carne
—en cuya piel se demostraba cómo,
contra lo que pudiera suponerse,
hay cosas que mejora
la dieta anteriormente reseñada—.
Exhibían el oro en su sonrisa
(irresistible cuanto mas dorada)
y se morían casi siempre pronto,
viejos joviales de adorable prótesis
y desastrosa próstata
                    —la sífilis
no era asunto sencillo en aquel tiempo.
Venían generalmente de La Habana.

Yo ignoraba, en los años

SECOND EVOCATION

I remember the *Indianos**
of my childhood.
We were told they were good people.
They donated public fountains
and schools to the villages
from where
hunger had
expelled them when they were children
from their weak, nutritive refuge,
protected
from tuberculosis
only by corn and potatoes.
They also donated brilliant chalices
of gold to the churches,
radiant crowns
to the virgins of wood, and valuable coins
to the other virgins: those of the flesh
—whose skin proved,
against whatever could be assumed,
that some things are improved
by the diet that I've just mentioned—.
They would show off the gold in their smiles
(the more gold the more irresistible)
and they would almost always die quickly,
jovial old men with adorable prosthesis
and disastrous prostates
                                    —in their time
syphillis was no simple matter.
They generally came from Havana.

In those distant years

---

*Spaniards who left Spain to seek their fortune and returned to Spain poorer than when they left.

lejanos que hoy evoco,
los más elementales rudimentos
de Economía Política,
y no estaba a mi alcance, por lo tanto,
comprender los efectos y las causas
de aquella, en cualquier caso, generosa
conducta: hasta qué punto
tantas escuelas, fuentes y campanas,
todos esos molares e incisivos
de veintidós quilates,
tanta virgen,
oscurecían, lejos,
aquel paisaje opuesto de palmeras y cañas
de donde procedían,
secaban
en un lugar distante lo que reverdecían
en esta tierra nuestra, eran
aquí rumor y más allá silencio,
llanto remoto, muerte desterrada.
No obstante la ignorancia referida,
aquel infantil yo ahora evocado
ya entonces admiraba especialmente
a los que regresaban desprovistos
de todo resplandor:
los que traían
únicamente un resto de fatiga
entre las manos,
un equipaje sólo de nostalgia,
un patrimonio inútil de recuerdos
y el brillo del fracaso en la mirada
iluminando casi
una sonrisa apenas de tristeza.

that I recall
I ignored the more elementary
rudiments of Political Economics,
and it was not within my grasp then
to understand the causes and effects
of such, can we say, generous conduct:
to what extent all those schools,
fountains and bells,
all the molars and incisors
of twenty-two carats,
so many virgins,
that contrary landscape, darkened, obscured
and faraway, of palm trees and sugar cane
they were coming from,
dried-up
in a distant place that they made blossom again
in this land of ours, they were
just a rumor and further away silence,
remote tears, death uprooted.
In spite of my previously mentioned ignorance,
that "innocent" that I now evoke
especially admired already
the ones that came back deprived
of all splendor:
the ones that brought
between their hands
only the remains of fatigue,
a luggage made only of nostalgia,
a useless patrimony of memories
and the brilliance of failure in their glances,
scarcely illuminating,
and smiles scarcely sad.

PRIMERA EVOCACIÓN

Recuerdo
bien
a mi madre.
Tenía miedo del viento,
era pequeña
de estatura,
la asustaban los truenos,
y las guerras
siempre estaba temiéndolas
de lejos,
desde antes
de la última ruptura
del Tratado suscrito
por todos los ministros de asuntos exteriores.

Recuerdo
que yo no comprendía.
El viento se llevaba
silbando
las hojas de los árboles,
y era como un alegre barrendero
que dejaba las niñas
despeinadas y enteras,
con las piernas desnudas e inocentes.

Por otra parte, el trueno
tronaba demasiado, era imposible
soportar sin horror esa estridencia,
aunque jamás ocurría nada luego:
la lluvia se encargaba de borrar
el dibujo violento del relámpago
y el arco iris ponía
un bucólico fin a tanto estrépito.

FIRST EVOCATION

I remember
my mother
so very well.
She was small
and afraid of the wind,
thunder frightened her too,
and wars,
even if very far away,
she always feared them,
even before
the last broken treaty
signed by all
the secretaries of state.

I remember
I didn't understand.
The wind whistled
as it swept
leaves from the trees,
it was the happy street sweeper
that left the young girls
tousled but firm
with bare and innocent legs.

On the other hand, the thunder
thundered too much, it was impossible
to endure that harshness without horror,
even if nothing ever happened afterwards:
the rain would erase
the lightning's violent outline
and a rainbow would put
a bucolic end to all that noise.

One evil summer war also came.

Llegó también la guerra un mal verano.
Llegó después la paz, tras un invierno
todavía peor. Esa vez, sin embargo,
no devolvió lo arrebatado el viento.
Ni la lluvia
pudo borrar las huellas de la sangre.
Perdido para siempre lo perdido,
atrás quedó definitivamente
muerto lo que fue muerto.

Por eso (y por más cosas)
recuerdo muchas veces a mi madre:

cuando el viento
se adueña de las calles de la noche,
y golpea las puertas, y huye, y deja
un rastro de cristales y de ramas
rotas, que al alba
la ciudad muestra desolada y lívida;

cuando el rayo
hiende el aire, y crepita,
y cae en tierra,
trazando surcos de carbón y fuego,
erizando los lomos de los gatos
y trastocando el norte de las brújulas;

y, sobre todo, cuando
la guerra ha comenzado,
lejos—nos dicen—y pequeña
—no hay por qué preocuparse—, cubriendo
de cadáveres mínimos distantes territorios,
de crímenes lejanos, de huérfanos pequeños . . .

Then after a winter that was
even worse, peace came. This time, however,
the wind didn't bring back what had been swept away.
Nor could the rain
wash away traces of blood.
What was lost was gone forever,
what was dead remained dead
for all of eternity.

For these (and for other things)
I often remember my mother:

when the wind
takes up its ownership of the streets at night
and beats at the doors, and flees, and leaves
behind a trail of broken windowpanes
and branches, which the city,
desolate and livid, displays at dawn;

when a lightning bolt
splits the air and crackles,
and falls to the earth,
tracing coal black furrows of fire,
making cats' hair stand on end,
and upsetting the magnetic north;

and above all else, when
war has begun,
far away—we're told—and it's a little
one at that—it's nothing to worry about—covering
distant lands with tiny corpses,
distant crimes, small orphans . . .

BREVES ACOTACIONES PARA UNA BIOGRAFIA

1969

BRIEF MARGINAL NOTES FOR A BIOGRAPHY

1969

A VECES

Escribir un poema se parece a un orgasmo:
mancha la tinta tanto como el semen,
empreña también más, en ocasiones.
Tardes hay, sin embargo,
en las que manoseo las palabras,
muerdo sus senos y sus piernas ágiles,
les levanto las faldas con mis dedos,
las miro desde abajo,
les hago lo de siempre
y, pese a todo, ved:

                no pasa nada.

Lo expresaba muy bien César Vallejo:
Lo digo, y no me corro.

Pero él disimulaba.

SOMETIMES

To create a poem is like having an orgasm:
ink stains just like semen,
and, occasionally, it impregnates better.
However, there are afternoons
when I fool around with words,
biting their breasts and agile legs,
lifting their skirts with my fingers,
looking at them from underneath,
I do to them what I always do
and, despite this, look:
nothing happens.

César Vallejo expressed it best:
I say it, and I cannot come.

But he was just pretending.

SIEMPRE LO QUE QUIERAS

Cuando tengas dinero regálame un anillo,
cuando no tengas nada dame una esquina de tu boca,
cuando no sepas qué hacer vente conmigo
—pero luego no digas que no sabes lo que haces.

Haces haces de leña en las mañanas
y se te vuelven flores en los brazos.
Yo te sostengo asida por los pétalos,
como te muevas te arrancaré el aroma.

Pero ya te lo dije:
cuando quieras marcharte ésta es la puerta:
se llama Ángel y conduce al llanto.

WHATEVER YOU WANT

When you have money, buy me a ring,
when you have nothing, give me a corner of your mouth,
when you don't know what to do, come with me
—but later don't say you didn't know what you were doing.

In the morning you gather bundles of firewood
and they turn into flowers in your arms.
I hold you up grasping the petals,
if you leave I'll take away your perfume.

But I've already told you:
if you decide to leave, here's the door:
its name is Ángel and it leads to tears.

MERIENDO ALGUNAS TARDES

Meriendo algunas tardes:
no todas tienen pulpa comestible.

Si estoy junto a la mar
muerdo primero los acantilados.
luego las nubes cárdenas y el cielo
—escupo las gaviotas—,
y para postre dejo las bañistas
jugando a la pelota y despeinadas.

Si estoy en la ciudad
meriendo tarde a secas:
mastico lentamente los minutos
—tras haberles quitado las espinas—
y cuando se me acaban
me voy rumiando sombras,
rememorando el tiempo devorado
con un acre sabor a nada en la garganta.

I SNACK ON SOME AFTERNOONS

I snack on some afternoons:
but not every one has edible pulp.

If I'm close to the sea
I first bite the cliffs,
then the purple clouds and the sky
—I spit out the sea gulls—,
and for dessert I leave the sunbathers
disheveled and playing ball.

If I'm in the city
I snack on just dry afternoons:
I slowly chew minutes
—after first removing their bones—
and when I'm finished,
I leave gnawing shadows,
remembering the eaten time
with a bitter taste of nothing in my throat.

MI VOCACIÓN PROFUNDA

Yo buceo debajo de las cosas.
La gente dice: buzo,
y yo emerjo desde el fondo de las mesas,
chorreando tallarines como un tritón de alcoba.

Una vez crucé un año debajo de los días.
Cuando llegué de nuevo al mes de enero
tuvieron que hacerme la respiración boca a boca.
Me dio tanto asco que volví a sumergirme.

Nada hay comparable, sin embargo,
al gozo inoxidable de trocearse en dedos,
narices, ojos, penes, labios, cabellos, risas,
y refugiarse en vasos individuales llenos
de ginebra con menta
hasta que alguien nos diga agitando banderas:

comencemos de nuevo;
la guerra ha terminado con el triunfo de mayo.

MY PROFOUND VOCATION

I dive underneath things.
People say: diver,
and I emerge from beneath the tables,
gushing noodles like a bedroom newt.

I once passed under the days of an entire year.
When I arrived again at January
they had to give me mouth-to-mouth resuscitation.
I felt so revolted I submerged again.

However, there's nothing comparable
to the stainless joy of slicing oneself into fingers,
noses, eyes, penises, lips, hair, laughter,
and taking refuge in individual glasses
of gin with mint
until someone, shaking flags, says to us:

> *let's begin anew;*
> *the war has ended with the triumph of May.*

HOY

Hoy todo me conduce a su contrario:
el olor de la rosa me entierra en sus raíces,
el despertar me arroja a un sueño diferente,
existo, luego muero.

Todo sucede ahora en un orden estricto:
los alacranes comen en mis manos,
las palomas me muerden las entrañas,
los vientos más helados me encienden las mejillas.

Hoy es así mi vida.
Me alimento del hambre.
Odio a quien amo.

Cuando me duermo, un sol recién nacido
me mancha de amarillo los párpados por dentro.

Bajo su luz, cogidos de la mano,
tú y yo retrocedemos desandando los días
hasta que al fin logramos perdernos en la nada.

TODAY

Today everything leads me to its contrary:
the odor of the rose inters me in its origins,
waking up throws me into a different dream,
I exist, therefore I die.

Now, everything follows in an exact order:
the scorpion eats from my hands,
the doves murder the innermost parts of me,
the ever colder winds ignite my cheeks.

Today my life is just like that.
Hunger nourishes me.
I hate the one I love.

When I fall asleep a newborn sun
stains the inside of my eyelids yellow.

Hand in hand, beneath its light,
you and I turn back to retrace the days
until, finally, we are lost in nothingness.

PROCEDIMIENTOS NARRATIVOS

1972

NARRATIVE PROCEDURES

1972

DEL CAMPO O DE LA MAR

Huimos con nuestros enseres y nos dispersamos por
    los campos,
buscando preferentemente las orillas del mar y de los
    ríos.
(Dejamos atrás la desolación, el sufrimiento,
la ciudad desierta y calcinada.)
No sabíamos qué hacer en las mañanas
y marisqueábamos despacio por los acantilados
o, tumbados bajo el sol,
dejábamos que el tiempo planease sobre nuestras
    cabezas
—tenaz y lento como un buitre—
nuestra futura destrucción, quizá inminente.
Thelonius Monk, Vivaldi y otros monstruos
nos roían las entrañas, percutían
en nuestras visceras, colmaban
los cuerpos de deseo, de sed de alcohol, de angustia por
    las tardes,
y la noche nos expulsaba con violencia fuera de nuestros
    refugios.
Impulsados por algo parecido al miedo,
acudíamos entonces en busca de otros rostros,
gentes de todo el mundo compartían nuestra urgencia,
acosados por ritmos y canciones
—el *rock* igual que un látigo cruzándonos el pecho—,
donde quiera que fueras Bob Dylan te encontraba.
Estábamos seguros de que todo era inútil,
mirarse, sonreír, hablar incluso,
besar, amar, nada nos salvaría.
Nadie se salvará,
nosotros mismos
nos entregamos, dóciles:

OF THE FIELD OR SEA

We fled with our possessions and scattered
       through the fields,
most of us flocking to the riverbanks
       and seashore.
(We left behind desolation, suffering,
the city deserted and burnt to ashes.)
We didn't know what to do in the mornings,
so we slowly searched through the cliffs for shellfish
or, lazing under the sun,
let time glide over our
        heads
—slow and tenacious as a vulture—
our future destruction imminent, perhaps.
Thelonius Monk, Vivaldi and other monsters
ate away at our insides, beat in
our guts, our bodies
overflowing with desire, a craving for alcohol, an anxiety
       all through the long afternoons,
and then the night drove us
       from our refuges.
Driven by something similar to fear,
we went in search of other faces,
people from all over the world shared our urgency,
pursued by rhythms and songs
—rock music just like a whip across the chest—,
and wherever you went Bob Dylan found you.
We were sure that everything was useless:
that to gaze at each other, to smile, to kiss,
to love, even to speak, nothing could save us.
No one will be saved,
we surrendered
ourselves dociley:

era imposible resistir más tiempo.
El regreso fue largo y doloroso.

La carretera estaba intransitable,
había policías en los cruces,
subimos a los trenes atestados,
los niños pedían agua,
las mujeres mostraban sus muslos sin malicia,
indiferentes, fatigados, sucios
—no había donde sentarse—,
así llegamos.

Perdida la costumbre, los asombrados ojos
trataban de orientarse penetrando las ruinas.

El otoño oxidaba la ciudad y sus parques.

Definitivamente,
el veraneo había terminado.

it was impossible to resist any longer.
The return was long and painful.

The highways were intransient,
policemen at all the crossroads,
so we boarded the overcrowded trains,
children begged for water,
women innocently revealed their thighs,
indifferent, tired, dirty
—there was no place to sit—,
this is how we arrived.

Having become disoriented, astonished eyes
tried to orientate themselves by penetrating the ruins.

Autumn was oxidizing the cities and their parks.

Definitely,
summer vacation had come to an end.

REALISMO MÁGICO

Ese médium marica
                (y si lo llamo
así, no es porque fuese
un poco afeminado—que lo era—,
sino porque, además de otros contactos,
tenía relación con los espíritus.
Pero en fin, a lo nuestro:)
ese marica y médium me predijo
con ayuda del naipe
las peores desgracias para agosto.
Y realmente acertó.
                El as de bastos
reafirmó con su oscura contundencia
las raras conjunciones
de las espadas con las copas,
urdidas
para mi desventura
por el azar quizá o por el destino.
En resumen
salió torcido el mes, salió insidioso,
desviando
por rutas todavía más siniestras
el curso de los meses anteriores.
No me atrevo a decir
que ya nada peor puede ocurrirme,
porque aún estoy vivo y sé de sobra
todos los riesgos que el vivir implica.
Lo diría, no obstante, mas sucede
que me dan mucho miedo las barajas,
los panes invertidos, los saleros,
los paraguas abiertos en la alcoba,
Buda, Yahvé, Mahoma—vaya trío—,
todo lo que en la sombra manipula,
compromete, corrompe, traza, borra

MAGIC REALISM

That gay medium
                    (and if I call him
gay it's not that he was
even a little bit effeminate—although he was—
but that, in addition to other contacts,
he had dealings with the spirits.
But back to the business at hand:)
that fairy and medium predicted for me,
with the help of his cards,
the worst misfortunes for August.
And he certainly got that right.
                    The ace of clubs
reaffirmed with dark forcefulness
the rare union
of spades with hearts,
plotted
for my misfortune
perhaps by chance or destiny.
In other words
the month turned out twisted, insidious,
diverting
along even more sinister paths
the course of the preceding months.
I don't dare say
that nothing worse could happen to me now,
because I'm still alive and I know only too well
all the risks that simply living implies.
Even so I'll say this, as it happens
I'm afraid of playing cards,
upside-down loaves of bread, saltshakers,
umbrellas opened in the bedroom,
Buddha, Yahweh, Mohammed—what a trio—
everything that manipulates from the shadows,
everything that compromises, corrupts, traces, erases

el devenir de la existencia humana.
Por todo ello creo que lo sensato
será guardar silencio,
no sea que se irriten las tijeras,
o que el número trece caiga en martes,
o que el siete de espadas
—presidio u hospital es su designio—
me atrape entre sus rejas para siempre.

Para salir de trances tan amargos,
una pequeña mano haciendo la puñeta
llevo colgada al cuello, y la dirijo
al mundo y al trasmundo, a mí y a ustedes.

the future of human existence.
I think the sensible thing, for all of
these reasons, is to keep quiet,
let the scissors be annoyed,
let the thirteenth fall on Tuesday,
let the seven of spades
—its design, prison or hospital—
entrap me between its bars forever.

To avoid such bitter moments
I wear a little masturbating hand
that hangs around my neck and I point it
at the world and the afterworld, at myself and at each of you.

CIENCIA AFLICCIÓN

Si todo problema al resolverse plantea más problemas,
dentro de poco tiempo será difícil andar por las
    calles.
—*Guau, guau,*
nos dirán los problemas enseñándonos los dientes,
mordiéndonos los fondillos de los pantalones,
aturdiéndonos con sus bufonadas insolubles.

Si todo problema
—como viene sucediendo hasta ahora—
plantea dos problemas,
dentro de poco valdrá más morirse.
A los paracaidistas no se les abrirá el paracaídas,
los conductores no sabrán conducirse,
los rectores no regirán.
Los problemas son prolíficos como ratas
y hasta los cerebros electrónicos se estremecen en las
        noches de luna llena,
cuando una lívida lucidez ilumina los ficheros
donde las ecuaciones sonríen petulantes
afilando los ángulos de sus raíces cúbicas.

SCIENCE AS AFFLICTION

If every problem upon being resolved just turns into
    another problem,
it'll soon be hard to walk the streets.
"Woof, woof,"
the problems will say to us, baring their teeth,
biting the seat of our pants,
confusing us with their esoteric jokes.

If every problem
—as has happened up to now—
turns into two problems,
we'll soon be better off dead.
Parachutists' parachutes will not open,
conductors will not know how to conduct,
presidents will not preside.
Problems are as prolific as rats
and even the electronic brains shudder when
the moon is full,
when a livid lucidity illumines the filing cabinets
where equations smile petulantly,
sharpening the angles of their cubic roots.

PALABRAS DESPRENDIDAS DE PINTURAS DE
JOSÉ HERNÁNDEZ

1.—*Alborada*

Un gallo canta piedras:
amanece.

(Luna delgada, pálida, traslúcida,
con el cielo se funde, inmóvil, yerta.)

Contra las tejas,
contra los cristales,
un gallo canta sangre.

(El viento
zarandea a los árboles dormidos.)

Canta crestas un gallo,
canta agallas,
escupe sus mollejas contra el cielo.

(Por las laderas ruedan frutas verdes
precipitadas hacia los barrancos.)

Golpeando las puertas, las ventanas,
el gallo con su canto insiste, advierte.

(Los buitres en lo alto de las rocas
desentumecen sus enormes alas.)

Un gallo pone un surtidor de fuego
en el límite blanco de la noche.

Nada más puede hacer: grita, amenaza.

WORDS TAKEN FROM A PAINTING BY
JOSÉ HERNÁNDEZ

1.—The first light of day

A rooster sings stones:
daybreak.

(Thin, pallid, translucent moon,
immobile, rigid, fused with sky.)

Against the tiles,
against the glass,
a rooster sings blood.

                     (The wind
sifts through the sleeping trees.)

A rooster's song crests,
it sings gall-nuts,
spits its gizzard against the sky.

Green fruits spill down
the slopes into the ravines.

Knocking on doors, windows,
the rooster's insistent song warns you.

(Vultures high on the rocks
stretch their enormous wings.)

A rooster lays a stream of fire
across the white border of night.

Nothing else could happen: shouts, threats.

Anuncia que la tregua ha terminado.

2.—*Fin del último acto*

Qué grandioso final
                    la ópera acaba
se desploma
                    una ovación
parte de la tarima
                    estalla contra el muro
rasgando los papeles decorados
                    el telón no desciende
se abre, crece
                    casi visible un grito
una grieta
                    del último cantante
(lagarto de ceniza
                    permanece un momento
hormiguero de polvo
                    en la resplandeciente
araña
                    cristalina
invasora
                    nada
que llega a todas partes
                    deslizándose al fin
con sus flexibles patas
                    por la partida cúpula
desde la oscuridad más inquietante
                    a otra nada más amplia
la del cielo)
                    donde se desvanece para siempre.

Imprevista tristeza se desprende del techo,
manchando levemente

It's just been announced that the truce has ended.

2.—*End of the last act*

At the grand finale
>   *the opera is finished*
part of the platform
>   *an ovation*
collapses
>   *explodes against the wall*
tearing the paper decorations
>   *the curtain doesn't fall*
a crack
>   *an almost invisible cry*
appears, expands
>   *from the last singer*
(lizard of ash
>   *hangs for a moment*
ant-hill of dust
>   *in the shining*
an invading
>   *crystalline*
spider
>   *nothingness*
that reaches into everything
>   *sliding at last*
with its flexible forelegs
>   *through the divided cupola*
from the sky's most frightening obscurity
>   *into another more amplified nothingness*
frightening obscurity
>   *where it disappears forever.*

An unforseen sadness breaks away from the roof
slightly stains

trajes, mármoles, flores, frentes, sombras.
Ya nada es como antes.
                              Ningún cuerpo regresa
a su ser verdadero.
                    Los ojos
no reconocen lo que buscan.
El hueco (que fue piedra
((la piedra que fue carne (((la carne
que fue grito ((((el grito que fue
¿amor, miedo, esperanza?)))))))
se agranda, se deforma,
estalla en mil pedazos de vacío
que golpean los rostros ya impasibles.

Frases voladas de unos labios mustios,
ecos de diálogos banales,
vagan por el vestíbulo desierto
como semillas secas suspensas en el aire

—*¿Dónde está la salida?*
—*Aún falta mucho para ayer.*
                              —*Perdone*
—*Pero el frío prosigue.*
                    —*No, no es nada.*

como el humo dormido de una hoguera extinguida,
que la brisa implacable deshace bruscamente.

the costumes, the marble, the flowers, foreheads, shadows.
Already nothing is like before.
                                No body returns
to their true self.
                    The eyes
can't recognize what they seek.
The emptiness (that was stone
((stone that was flesh (((flesh
that was a cry ((((cry that
was love, fear, hope?)))))))
is enlarged, deformed,
explodes into a thousand pieces of emptiness
that strikes the already impassive faces.

Phrases fly from gloomy lips,
echoes of banal dialogues
wander through the deserted lobby
like dry seeds suspended in the air

—*Where's the exit?*
—*Yesterday still lacks so much.*
                        —*Excuse me.*
But the cold follows.
                    —*No, it's nothing*

like the smoke asleep in an extinguished bonfire,
that the implacable breeze suddenly releases.

MUESTRA, CORREGIDA Y AUMENTADA, DE
ALGUNOS PROCEDIMIENTOS NARRATIVOS Y DE
LAS ACTITUDES SENTIMENTALES QUE
HABITUALMENTE COMPORTAN

1976

NARRATIVE PROCEDURES AND THE EMOTIONAL ATTITUDES THAT THEY USUALLY ENTAIL

1976

SONATA PARA VIOLÍN SOLO
(Juan Sebastián Bach)

Como la mano pura que graba en las paredes
mensajes obsesivos de amor,
sueños cifrados,
                    así
la trayectoria cruel de este cuchillo
me está marcando el alma.

Mas su caligrafía no es oscura
ni inocente:
                    bien claro deletrea
la obscenidad del tiempo, sus siniestros
designios.
                    ¡Qué desgracia!
                                        Ahora,
cuando salga a la calle,
cualquiera
podrá ver en mi rostro
—lo mismo que en las piedras profanadas
de un viejo templo en ruinas—
los nombres, los deseos, las fechas que componen
—abandonado todo a la intemperie—
el confuso perfil de un sueño roto,
el símbolo roído de una yerta esperanza.

SONATA FOR VIOLIN SOLO
(Johann Sebastian Bach)

Like a pure hand engraving on the walls
obsessive messages of love,
coded dreams,
                    just like that
the cruel trajectory of this knife
is carving my soul.

But its calligraphy is neither obscure
nor innocent:
                    the obscenity
of time so clearly spells its sinister
designs.
            What a disgrace!
                                Now,
when I go out to the street,
anyone
can see in my face
—just as in the profaned stones
of an old temple in ruins—
the names, desires, the dates that compose
—everything abandoned to the weather—
the confused profile of a broken dream,
the corroded symbol of a withered hope.

REVERBERA LA MÚSICA EN LOS MUROS

Reverbera la música en los muros
y traspasa mi cuerpo como si no existiese.

¿Soy sólo una memoria que regresa
desde el cabo remoto de la vida,
fiel a una invocación que no perdona?

Música que rechazan las paredes:
sólo soy eso.

Cuando ella cesa también yo me extingo.

THE MUSIC IN THE WALLS REVERBERATES

The music in the walls reverberates
and passes through my body as if it didn't exist.

Am I only a memory returning
from the remote end of life,
faithful to an invocation that doesn't forgive?

Music that the walls reject:
I am only that.

When it ceases I am also finished.

A VECES, EN OCTUBRE, ES LO QUE PASA

Cuando nada sucede,
y el verano se ha ido,
y las hojas comienzan a caer de los árboles
y el frío oxida el borde de los ríos
y hace más lento el curso de las aguas;

cuando el cielo parece un mar violento,
y los pájaros cambian de paisaje,
y las palabras se oyen cada vez más lejanas,
como susurros que dispersa el viento;

entonces,
ya se sabe,
es lo que pasa:

esas hojas, los pájaros, las nubes,
las palabras dispersas y los ríos,
nos llenan de inquietud súbitamente
y de desesperanza.

No busquéis el motivo en vuestros corazones.
Tan sólo es lo que dije:
lo que pasa.

SOMETIMES, IN OCTOBER, THAT'S WHAT HAPPENS

When nothing happens,
and summer has gone,
and leaves begin to fall from trees,
and cold rusts the edges of rivers,
and slows the flow of waters;

when the sky appears to be a violent sea,
and birds change the landscape,
and words are heard farther away each time,
like whispers scattered by the wind;

then,
we already know
that's what happens:

those leaves, the birds, the clouds,
the scattered words and rivers
suddenly fill us with restlessness
and hopelessness.

Don't search for the reason in your hearts.
It's just what I've told you:
that's what happens.

ESTOY BARTOK DE TODO

Estoy bartok de todo,
bela
bartok de ese violín que me persigue,
de sus fintas precisas,
de las sinuosas violas,
de la insidia que el oboe propaga,
de la admonitoria gravedad del fagot,
de la furia del viento,
del hondo crepitar de la madera.

Resuena bela en todo bartok: tengo
miedo.
      La música
ha ocupado mi casa.
Por lo que oigo,
puede ser peligrosa.
Échenla fuera.

I AM BARTOK OF EVERYTHING

I am bartok of everything
bela
bartok of this violin that pursues me,
of its precise feints,
of the sinuous violas,
of the insidiousness that the oboe propagates,
of the admonitory gravity of the bassoon,
of the wind's fury,
of the deep crackle of wood.

Resounds bela in all of bartok: I am
afraid.
      Music
has occupied my house.
From what I hear
it can be dangerous.
Throw it out.

HOROSCOPO PARA UN TIRANO OLVIDADO

Ni Mars
ni Venus:
sólo
Marte de carnaval,
sórdido Eros de café cantante,
con chistera al prostíbulo,
recién besada la mano de la reina.

En la tribuna,
presidiendo el desfile,
tu pecho rutilante de medallas y cruces
brilla como una noche constelada:
noche que alberga todas las traiciones.

Pero tú no podrás, no:
no pudiste.

Otro vendrá después que te hará bueno.

Asesino platónico,
tu idea
del crimen
será soberbiamente realizada,
y el desprecio
—el Norte de tus actos—
desde otra boca azuzará a la muerte
con más saña que tú y mejor fortuna.

Muere tranquilo y solo, desterrado,
si acaso te consuela saber esto:
en nuestros días
pocas veces los hombres su destino merecen;
también los justos que te combatieron
han de morirse desterrados, solos.

HOROSCOPE FOR A FORGOTTEN DICTATOR

Not Mars
nor Venus:
just
Mardi Gras,
sordid Eros of music halls,
with top hats to the whorehouse,
just after having kissed the queen's hand.

On the platform,
presiding over the parade,
your chest brilliant with medals and crosses
shines like a star-studded night:
a night that harbors all treasons.

But you wouldn't, no:
you couldn't.

After all, another will come along and make you look good.

Platonic murderer,
your idea
of crime
will be arrogantly carried out,
and the disdain
—North Star of your actions—
from another mouth will provoke death
with more rage and better luck than you.

Die in peace and alone, exiled.
It may comfort you to know:
in our day
rarely do men deserve their destiny:
also, the just who fought against you
will die exiled, alone.

OTRA VEZ

A Pablo Neruda y Salvador
Allende. In memoriam.

Sangre: no sangres más.
¡Cómo decirte que no sangres, sangre!
¿Nunca ha cesado de correr la sangre?

Contemplad el pasado
                    —esos *graffiti* obscenos:
la huella de una mano ensangrentada
en el muro sombrío de la Historia.

Y el presente:
                    más sangre,
otra vez sangre.
                    (Ahora
                         —el mensaje es la sangre—
un general con nombre de payaso
hace correr,
                    en Chile,
la triste gracia de la sangre:
la sangre de los justos,
la que redime al hombre del horror de ser hombre,
la sangre más valiosa, la más pura.)

Para que deje de correr la sangre
¿hará falta más sangre?
Tiempo largo, sangriento:
                                        derrama
la última gota de tu sangre, pronto.

No hay tiempo que llorar.

Cuando no sangre más así la sangre,
ese día, por fin, será el futuro.

AGAIN

*To Pablo Neruda and Salvador
Allende. In memoriam.*

Blood: don't bleed anymore.
How to tell you not to bleed, blood!
Has blood ever ceased to run?

Contemplate the past
                        —those obscene *graffiti:*
the bloody handprint
on the somber wall of History.

And the present:
                        more blood,
again, blood.
            (Now,
                        —blood is the message—
. a general with a clown's name
makes flow,
            in Chile,
the sad grace of blood:
the blood of the just,
that which redeems man from the horror of being man,
the most precious blood, the purest.)

To keep blood from running
will there have to be more blood?
Long, bloody time:
                        spill
the last drop of your blood, quick!

There's no time to cry.

When blood no longer bleeds,
that day, at last, will be the future.

231

POÉTICA
a la que intento a veces aplicarme.

Escribir un poema: marcar la piel del agua.
Suavemente, los signos
se deforman, se agrandan,
expresan lo que quieren
la brisa, el sol, las nubes,
se distienden, se tensan, hasta
que el hombre que los mira
—adormecido el viento,
la luz alta—
o ve su propio rostro
o—transparencia pura, hondo
fracaso—no ve nada.

POETICS
that I sometimes try to follow.

To write a poem: mark the water's skin.
Smoothly, the symbols
change shape, grow larger,
express what the breeze,
the sun, the clouds want,
swelling up, tightening up, until
the man who sees them
—drowsy wind,
high noon—
sees his own face
or—pure transparency, deep
failure—sees nothing.

ORDEN

Poética a la que otros se aplican.

Los poetas prudentes,
como las vírgenes—cuando las había—,
no deben separar los ojos
del firmamento.
¡Oh, tú, extranjero osado
que miras a los hombres:
contempla las estrellas!
(El Tiempo, no la Historia.)
Evita
la claridad obscena.
                          (Cave canem.)
Y edifica el misterio.
                          Sé puro:
no nombres; no ilumines.
Que tu palabra oscura se derrame en la noche
sombría y sin sentido
lo mismo que el momento de tu vida.

ORDER
Poetics that others follow.

Prudent poets,
like virgins—when such things existed—,
should not take their eyes off
heaven.
Oh, you, bold foreigner
who watches men:
contemplate the stars!
(Time, not History.)
Avoid
obscene clarity.
                    (Cave canem.)
And build mystery.
                    Be pure:
don't name; don't illuminate.
Let your obscure word flow into the night
shadowy and senseless
like this moment of your life.

CONTRA-ORDEN
Poética por la que me pronuncio ciertos días.

Esto es un poema.

Aquí está permitido
fijar carteles,
tirar escombros, hacer aguas
y escribir frases como:

Marica el que lo lea,
Amo a Irma,
Muera el . . . (silencio),
Arena gratis,
Asesinos,
etcétera.

Esto es un poema.
Mantén sucia la estrofa.
Escupe dentro.

Responsable la tarde que no acaba,
el tedio de este día,
la indeformable estolidez del tiempo.

COUNTER-ORDER
Poetics that I announce on certain days.

This is a poem.

Here it's okay
to put up posters,
throw trash, piss
and write phrases like:

Whoever reads this is a fag,
I love Irma,
Death to the . . . (silence),
Free sand,
Murderers,
etcetera.

This is a poem.
Keep the stanza dirty.
Spit into it.

Blame the endless afternoon,
the tedium of this day,
the unchanging stolidity of time.

A LA POESÍA

Ya se dijeron las cosas más oscuras.
También las más brillantes.
Ya se enlazaron las palabras como
cabellos, seda y oro en una misma trenza
—adorno de tu espalda transparente—.
Ahora,
tan bella como estás,
recién peinada,
quiero tomar de ti lo que más amo.
Quiero tomarte
—aunque soy viejo y pobre—
no el oro ni la seda:
tan sólo el simple, el fresco, el puro
(apasionadamente), el perfumado,
el leve (airadamente), el suave pelo.
Y sacarte a las calles,
despeinada,
ondulando en el viento
—libre, suelto, a su aire—
tu cabello sombrío
como una larga y negra carcajada.

The most obscure things have already been said.
Also the most brilliant.
Words already linked to each other like
hair, silk and gold in the same braid
—adorning your transparent back—.
Now,
as beautiful as you are,
your hair just brushed,
I want to take from you what I love the most.
I want from you
—even though I am old and poor—
neither gold nor silk:
just the simple, fresh, pure
(passionately), perfumed,
light (furiously), soft hair.
I want to take you out to the streets,
disheveled,
your dark hair
—free, loose, on its own—
undulating in the wind
like a long and loud black laughter.

ODA A LOS NUEVOS BARDOS

Mucho les importa la poesía.
Hablan constantemente de la poesía,
y se prueban metáforas como putas sostenes
ante el oval espejo de las *oes* pulidas
que la admiración abre en las bocas afines.

Aman la intimidad, sus interioridades
les producen orgasmos repentinos:
entreabren las sedas de su escote,
desatan cintas, desanudan lazos,
y misteriosamente,
con señas enigmáticas que el azar mitifica,
llaman a sus adeptos:
                    —*Mira mira* . . .

Detrás de las cortinas,
en el lujo en penumbra de los viejos salones
que los brocados doran con resplandor oscuro,
sus adiposidades brillan pálidamente
un instante glorioso.
                    Eso les basta.

Otras tardes de otoño reconstruyen
el esplendor de un tiempo desahuciado
por deudas impagables, perdido en la ruleta
de un lejano Casino junto a un lago
por el que se deslizan cisnes, *cisnes*
cuyo perfil

        —anotan sonrientes—

susurra, intermitente, eses silentes:
aliterada letra herida,
casi exhalada

ODE TO THE NEW BARDS

They care a lot about poetry.
They talk constantly of poetry,
and they try out metaphors like whores' bras
in front of the oval mirror of the polished *wows*
that admiration opens in sympathetic mouths.

They love intimacy, their private matters
produce for them sudden orgasms:
they half-open the silks of their décolletage,
untie ribbons, unknot knots,
and mysteriously
with enigmatic gestures that chance mystifies
they call to their followers:
                              —*look, look . . .*

Behind the curtains
in the dim luxury of old salons
that the brocades gild with dark glitter
their adiposity shines pallidly
for a glorious instant.
                    That is enough for them.

Other autumn afternoons they reconstruct
the splendor of a time exhausted
by unrepayable debts, lost in the roulette
of a distant Casino close to a lake
with gliding swans, *swans*
whose profile

                    —they note, smiling—

whispers, intermittently, those silent s's:
alliterated wounded letter,
almost sighed

—puesto que surgida
de la alerida pulcritud del ala—
en un S. O. S. que resbala
y que un peligro inadvertido evoca.
¡Y el cisne-cero-cisne que equivoca
al agua antes tranquila y ya alarmada,
era tan sólo nada-cisne-nada!

Pesados terciopelos sus éxtasis sofocan.

—since sprung from
the pure wing—
in an S.O.S. that glides
and that an unexpected danger evokes.
And that swan-zero-swan that mistakes
the once tranquil waters now ruffled,
was but nothing-swan-nothing!

Heavy velvets smother their ecstasies.

NOTAS DE UN VIAJERO

Siempre es igual aquí el verano:
sofocante y violento.
        Pero
hace muy pocos años todavía
este paisaje no era así.
        Era
más limpio y apacible—me cuentan—,
más claro, más sereno.

Ahora
el Imperio contrajo sus fronteras
y la resaca de una paz dudosa
arrastró a la metrópoli,
desde los más lejanos confines de la tierra,
un tropel pintoresco y peligroso:
aventureros, mercaderes,
soldados de fortuna, prostitutas, esclavos
recién manumitidos, músicos ambulantes,
falsos profetas, adivinos, bonzos,
mendigos y ladrones
que practican su oficio cuando pueden.

Todo el mundo amenaza a todo el mundo,
unos por arrogancia, otros por miedo.
Junto a las villas de los senadores,
insolentes hogueras
delatan la presencia de los bárbaros.
Han llegado hasta aquí con sus tambores,
asan carne barata al aire libre, cantan
canciones aprendidas en sus lejanas islas.
No conmemoran nada: rememoran,
repiten ritmos, sueños y palabras

A TRAVELER'S NOTES

Summer here is always the same:
suffocating and violent.
                                    But
a very few years ago,
the landscape was not yet like this.
                                    It was
cleaner and calmer—they tell me—,
clearer, more serene.

Now,
the Empire has shrunk its borders
and the hangover of a doubtful peace
has dragged to the metropolis,
from the most remote corners of the earth,
a picturesque and dangerous crowd:
adventurers, merchants,
soldiers of fortune, prostitutes, just-freed
slaves, street musicians,
street prophets, fortune-tellers, Buddhist monks,
beggars and thieves
who practice their trade when they can.

Everyone threatens everyone else,
some out of arrogance, some from fear.
Next to the senators' mansions,
insolent bonfires
betray the presence of the barbarians.
They have arrived here with their drums,
they roast cheap meat in the open air, they sing
songs learned on their distant islands.
They commemorate nothing: they remember,
they repeat rhythms, dreams and words

que muy pronto
perderán su sentido.

Traidores a su pueblo,
               desterrados
por su traición,
despreciados
por quienes los acogen con disgusto
tras haberlos usado sin provecho,
acaso un día
sea ésta la patria de sus hijos;
nunca la de ellos.
Su patria es esa música tan sólo,
el humo y la nostalgia
que levantan su fuego y sus canciones.

Cerca del Capitolio
hay tonsurados monjes mendicantes,
embadurnados de ceniza y púrpura,
que predican y piden mansamente
atención y monedas.
Orgullosos negros,
ayer todavía esclavos,
miran a las muchachas de tez clara
con sonrisa agresiva,
y escupen cuando pasan los soldados.
(Por mucho menos los ahorcaban antes.)

Desde sus pedestales,
los Padres de la Patria contemplan desdeñosos
el corruptor efecto de los días
sobre la gloria que ellos acuñaron.
Ya no son más que piedra o bronce, efigies,
perfiles en monedas, tiempo ido
igual que sus vibrantes palabras, convertidas

that very soon
will make no sense.

Traitors to their country,
                    exiled
for treason,
scorned
by those who receive them with disgust
after having used them without success,
maybe someday
this will be the land of their children;
never their own.
Their land is only that lonely music,
smoke and nostalgia
that rises from their fires and songs.

Next to the capitol,
tonsured and begging monks,
smeared with purple and ash,
preach and meekly beg for
attention and coins.
Proud negroes,
slaves just yesterday,
stare at the fair-skinned girls
with aggressive smiles,
and spit when the soldiers pass by.
(In the past they were hanged for less.)

From their pedestals,
the Fathers of the Country disdainfully contemplate
the corrupting effect of time
upon the glory they've coined.
Now they are only stone or bronze, effigies,
profiles on coins, like their vibrant
words, a time past, converted

en letra muerta que decora
los mármoles solemnes en su honor erigidos.

El aire huele a humo y a magnolias.
Un calor húmedo asciende de la tierra,
y el viento se ha parado.
En la ilusoria paz del parque juegan
niños en español.
Por el río Potomac remeros perezosos
buscan la orilla en sombra de la tarde.

into the dead letters that decorate
the solemn marble erected in their honor.

The air reeks of smoke and magnolias.
A humid heat rises from the earth,
and the wind has stopped.
In the illusory peace of the park, children
play in Spanish.
On the Potomac River lazy oarsmen
search for the shore in the shadow of the afternoon.

TEXAS, OTOÑO, UN DÍA

I.

¡Qué fragor el del sol contra los árboles!
Se agita todo el monte en verde espuma.
El aire es una llama transparente
que enciende y no consume
lo que sus lenguas lúcidas abrazan.
Por la profundidad turbia del cielo,
ánades cruzan en bandadas, hondos:
pétalos de la Rosa de los Vientos
que—¿hacia dónde, hacia dónde?—
los vientos caprichosos arrebatan.
Desde
las zarzas crepitantes de luz y mariposas,
la voz de un dios me exige
que sacrifique aquello que más amo.

II.

Pero tú nada temas:
pese a tanta belleza,
el deseo
de hallar la paz en el olvido
no prevalecerá contra tu imagen.

A FALL DAY, TEXAS

I.

What a clamor of sun against the trees!
The entire mountain shakes like green foam.
The air is a transparent flame
that burns without consuming
what its lucid tongues embrace.
Through the turbid breadth of the sky,
in its depths, geese cross in flocks:
petals of the Rose of the Winds
—bound for where? Where?—
that the capricious winds blow away.
From
brambles crackling with light and butterflies
the voice of a god demands
that I sacrifice what I love most.

II.

But fear nothing:
despite so much beauty,
the desire
to find peace in oblivion
will not prevail against your image.

Con tan inconsistentes materiales

—luz en polvo,
una tela de araña,
las ramas de un arbusto,
espacio, soledad, pájaros, viento—

ante mis ojos
levantó la tarde
un monumento de belleza
que parecía inextinguible:

inmensos pabellones de silencio,
galerías abiertas a altísimos abismos,
columnas de reflejos deslumbrantes,
lienzos tersos, ingrávidos,
de metal transparente como vidrio.

Mas todo aquello
                    —estatua o fortaleza—,
después de haberse erguido,
abrió dos grandes alas de misterio,
y se perdió en un velo negro y rápido.

De su presencia lúcida
sólo nos queda ahora
un desolado pedestal vacío
de sombra, y frío, y noche, y desamparo.

ACOMA, NEW MEXICO, DECEMBER, 5:15 P.M.

With such flimsy materials

—light in dust,
a spider's web,
the branches of a shrub,
space, solitude, birds, wind—

the afternoon lifted up
before my eyes
a monument of beauty
that seemed inextinguishable:

immense pavilions of silence,
balconies open to lofty abysses,
columns of dazzling reflections,
smooth, weightless canvases
of metal as transparent as glass.

But all of that
                    —statue or fortress—,
after having been erected,
spread two great wings of mystery,
and was lost in a black, rapid flight.

Of its gleaming presence
there remains for us only
a desolate, empty pedestal
of shadow, and cold, and night, and helplessness.

PROSEMAS O MENOS

1985

PROSEMS OR LESS

1985

EL DÍA SE HA IDO

Ahora andará por otras tierras,
llevando lejos luces y esperanzas,
aventando bandadas de pájaros remotos,
y rumores, y voces, y campanas,
—ruidoso perro que menea la cola
y ladra ante las puertas entornadas.

(Entretanto, la noche, como un gato
sigiloso, entró por la ventana,
vio unos restos de luz pálida y fría,
y se bebió la última taza.)

Sí;
        definitivamente el día se ha ido.
Mucho no se llevó (no trajo nada);
sólo un poco de tiempo entre los dientes,
un menguado rebaño de luces fatigadas.
Tampoco lo lloréis. Puntual e inquieto,
sin duda alguna, volverá mañana.
Ahuyentará a ese gato negro.
Ladrará hasta sacarme de la cama.

Pero no será igual. Será otro día.

Será otro perro de la misma raza.

THE DAY HAS GONE

By now it's walking through other lands,
carrying away lights and hopes,
scattering flocks of distant birds,
rumors, voices, and bells,
—a noisy dog wagging its tail
and barking at half-open doors.

(Meanwhile, night, like a stealthy
cat, entered through the window,
saw the pale, cold leftover light
and drank the last cup.)

Yes;
         the day has definitely gone.
It didn't carry away much (it didn't bring anything);
just a little time between its teeth,
a stunted flock of tired lights.
Don't cry for it. Punctual and restless,
no doubt, it will return tomorrow.
It will frighten away that black cat.
It will bark until it drags me out of bed.

But it won't be the same. It will be another day.

Another dog of the same breed.

ASÍ FUERON

La mañana
            —ese tigre
de papel de periódico—
ruge entre mis manos.

Ambigua e indecisa,
exhibiendo las fauces irascibles
en un largo bostezo,
se levanta:

va a abrevar en los ríos,
a teñirlos de rojo con sus barbas sangrientas.
Luego se precipita sobre el valle.

Las tres en punto ya;
parece que la luz, zarpa retráctil,
abandona su presa.

Pero eso,
            ¿quién lo sabe?

Agazapado
como una loba,
el crepúsculo espera
a que salga la luna
para aullar largamente.

Así fueron los días que recuerdo.

Los otros,
los que olvido
            —¡tengo ya tantos años!—
huyeron como corzas malheridas.

THE DAYS WERE LIKE THAT

Morning
    —that
newspaper tiger—
roars in my hands.

Ambiguous and undecided,
showing its irascible jaws
in a long yawn,
it gets up:

it goes to drink from the rivers,
staining them red with its bloody whiskers.
Then it leaps on the valley.

Three o'clock already;
the light, a retractile claw,
appears to abandon its prey.

But,
    who knows?

Twilight,
crouched like a wolf,
waits for the moon
to come out
to begin its long howl.

The days I remember were like that.

The others,
the ones I forget
—I'm already so old!—
fled like wounded deer.

CREPÚSCULO, ALBUQUERQUE, ESTÍO

¡Sol sostenido en el poniente, alta
polifonía de la luz!

Desde el otro confín del horizonte,
la montaña coral
—madera y viento—
responde con un denso acorde cárdeno
a la larga cadencia de la tarde.

TWILIGHT, ALBUQUERQUE, SUMMER

Sunlight sustained in the west, high
polyphony of light!

From the other side of the horizon,
the choral mountain
—wood and wind—
responds with a dense and purple chord
to the long cadence of evening.

CREPÚSCULO, ALBUQUERQUE, OTOÑO

En la distancia, el horizonte
arde:
  llama.

Responde la montaña con un largo
vagido intermitente:
      eco que quema,
brasa.

El valle,
entre dos fuegos.

Un silencio de sombras se adelanta
—frío reptil de ceniza—
oprimiendo la luz con sus escamas
grises.
   Quedan
en las cumbres rescoldos todavía,
humo y ascuas
a las que el viento arranca heladas chispas
que—ya todo acabado—
brillan allá en lo hondo, arriba, altas.

TWILIGHT, ALBUQUERQUE, FALL

In the distance, the horizon
blazes:
      calls.

The mountain responds with a long
intermittent wail:
            echo that burns,
red coal.

The valley,
between two fires.

A silence of shadows advances
—cold reptile of ash—
crushing the light with its gray
scales.
      Still
on the summit embers remain,
smoke and embers,
from which the wind snatches frozen sparks
that—everything already gone—
shine there, in the depths, above.

CREPÚSCULO, ALBUQUERQUE, INVIERNO

No fue un sueño,
lo vi:

La nieve ardía.

TWILIGHT, ALBUQUERQUE, WINTER

It wasn't a dream,
I saw it:

The snow was burning.

El llamado crepúsculo
¿no es el rubor—efímero—del día
que se siente culpable
por todo lo que fue
—y lo que no ha sido?

Ese día fugaz
que, igual que un delincuente,
aprovecha las sombras para irse.

THE SO-CALLED TWILIGHT

The so-called twilight,
is it not the blush—ephemeral—of the day
that feels guilty
for all it was
—and for all that it wasn't?

Fugitive day
that, like a thief,
takes advantage of the shadows to flee.

ROSA DE ESCÁNDALO

(Albuquerque, noviembre)

Súbita, inesperada, espesa nieve
ciega el último oro
de los bosques.
Un orden nuevo y frío
sucede a la opulencia del otoño.
Troncos indiferentes.
Silencio dilatado en muertos ecos.
Sólo los cuervos
protestan en voz alta,
descienden a los valles
y—airados e insolentes—
ocupan los jardines
con su negro equipaje de plumas y graznidos.
Inquietantes, incómodos, severos,
desde sus altos púlpitos marchitos
increpan a la tarde de noviembre
que exhibe todavía
entre sus galas secas
la belleza impasible de una rosa.

THE SCANDALOUS ROSE

(Albuquerque, November)

Suddenly, thick, unexpected snow
blinds the last gold
of the woods.
A new and cold order
succeeds the opulence of autumn.
Indifferent tree trunks.
Silence dilated in dead echoes.
In high voices,
only the ravens protest
as they descend into the valley
—angry and insolent—
and occupy the gardens
with their black luggage of plumage and squawks.
Disquieting, inconvenient, severe,
from their high and withered pulpits
they rebuke the November afternoon
that still exhibits
among its elegant drought
the impassive beauty of a single rose.

REVELACIÓN

Dios existe en la música.
En el centro
de la polifonía
se abre su reino inmenso y deslumbrante.
Incesante, infinita,
la creación extiende sus fronteras.
¿Qué improbable
constelación
se atrevería a brillar
más allá de sus límites?
Escalas luminosas tienden puentes
de firmamento a firmamento,
fundan el poderío
de la evidencia.
                    Asombro.
Es la verdad:
                    ¡Dios existe
en la música!

(Cuatro compases más, y otra vez solos.)

REVELATION

God exists in music.
In the center
of polyphony
His immense and dazzling heaven opens.
Incessantly, infinitely,
creation extends its borders.
Which unlikely
constellation
would dare to shine
beyond its limits?
Luminous scales extend bridges
from firmament to firmament,
forging the power
of proof.
           Astonishment.
It's true:
           God exists
in music!

(Four more beats, and alone again.)

EL CRISTO DE VELÁZQUEZ

A Luis Ríus

Banderillero desganado.
Las guedejas del sueño cubren tu ojo derecho.
Te quedaste dormido con los brazos alzados,
y un derrote de Dios te ha atravesado el pecho.

Un piadoso pincel lavó con leves
algodones de luz tu carne herida,
y otra vez la apariencia de la vida
a florecer sobre tu piel se atreve.

No burlaste a la muerte. No pudiste.
El cuerno y el pincel, confabulados,
dejaron tu derrota confirmada.

Fue una aventura absurda, bella y triste,
que aún estremece a los aficionados:
¡qué cornada, Dios mío, qué cornada!

THE CHRIST OF VELÁZQUEZ

To Luis Ríus

The half-hearted banderillo.
Long locks of dream hair cover your right eye.
You slept with raised arms
while a God-willed defeat pierced your chest.

A pious paintbrush washed your
wounded flesh with cottons of light,
and again the appearance of life
dares to flower upon your skin.

You didn't deceive death. You couldn't.
The horn and the paintbrush, schemers,
they confirmed your defeat.

It was an absurd adventure, beautiful and sad,
that still inspires the masses:
but that goring, my God, that goring!

Note: The title refers to *Christ on the Cross* (1631-32), a famous painting by Diego Velázquez (1599-1660).

DIATRIBA CONTRA LOS MUERTOS

Los muertos son egoístas:
hacen llorar y no les importa,
se quedan quietos en los lugares más inconvenientes,
se resisten a andar, hay que llevarlos
a cuestas a la tumba
como si fuesen niños, qué pesados.
Inusitadamente rígidos, sus rostros
nos acusan de algo, o nos advierten;
son la mala conciencia, el mal ejemplo,
lo peor de nuestra vida son ellos siempre, siempre.
Lo malo que tienen los muertos
es que no hay forma de matarlos.
Su constante tarea destructiva
es por esa razón incalculable.
Insensibles, distantes, tercos, fríos,
con su insolencia y su silencio
no se dan cuenta de lo que deshacen.

DIATRIBE AGAINST THE DEAD

The dead are selfish:
they make us cry and don't care,
they stay quiet in the most inconvenient places,
they refuse to walk, we have to carry them
on our backs to the tomb
as if they were children. What a burden!
Unusually rigid, their faces
accuse us of something, or warn us;
they are the bad conscience, the bad example,
they are the worst things in our lives always, always.
The bad thing about the dead
is that there is no way you can kill them.
Their constant destructive labor
is for that reason incalculable.
Insensitive, distant, obstinate, cold,
with their insolence and their silence
they don't realize what they undo.

AVANZABA DE ESPALDAS AQUEL RÍO

Avanzaba de espaldas aquel río.

No miraba adelante, no atendía
a su Norte—que era el Sur.
Contemplaba los álamos
altos, llenos de sol, reverenciosos,
perdiéndose despacio cauce arriba.
Se embebía en los cielos
cambiantes
del otoño:
                    decía adiós a su luz.
Retenía un instante las ramas de los sauces
en sus espumas frías,
para dejarlas irse—o sea, quedarse—,
mojadas y brillantes, por la orilla.
En los remansos
demoraba su marcha,
absorto ante el crepúsculo.

No ignoraba al mar ácido, tan próximo
que ya en el viento su rumor se oía.
Sin embargo,
continuaba avanzando de espaldas aquel río,
y se ensanchaba
para tocar las cosas que veía:
los juncos últimos,
la sed de los rebaños,
las blancas piedras por su afán pulidas,
Si no podía alcanzarlo,
lo acariciaba todo con sus ojos de agua.

¡Y con qué amor lo hacía!

THAT RIVER RAN BACKWARDS

That river ran backwards.

It didn't look forward, it didn't pay attention
to its North—that was its South.
It was contemplating the high
poplars, filled with sun, reverential,
getting slowly lost upstream.
Saturating itself with the changing
fall
sky:
            saying good-bye to its light.
Holding on for an instant,
in its cold foam, to the willows
and then letting go—that's to say, staying—,
wet and brilliant, along the bank.
Captivated by the twilight,
it delayed its journey
in the eddies.

It didn't ignore the bitter sea, so close
that its roar was blowing in the wind.
However,
the river continued going backwards,
stretching out
to touch what it saw:
the last rushes,
the thirsty flocks,
the white stones polished by its fervor.
What the river couldn't reach
it caressed with its watery eyes.

And did it with so much love!

ERUDITOS EN CAMPUS

Son los que son.

Apacibles, pacientes, divagando
en pequeños rebaños
por el recinto ajardinado,
                              vedlos.
O mejor, escuchadlos:

mugen difusa ciencia,
comen hojas de Plinio
y de lechuga,
devoran hamburguesas,
textos griegos,
diminutos textículos en sánscrito,
                              y luego
fertilizan la tierra
con clásicos detritus:
                    alma mater.

Si eructan,
un erudito dictum
perfuma el campus de sabiduría.

Si, silentes, meditan,
raudos, indescifrables silogismos,
iluminando un universo puro,
recorren sus neuronas fatigadas.
Buscan
—la mirada perdida en el futuro—
respuesta a los enigmas
eternos:

¿Qué salario tendré dentro de un año?
¿Es jueves hoy?
                    ¿Cuánto
tardará en derretirse tanta nieve?

ERUDITES ON CAMPUS

They are who they are.

Affable, patient, rambling
in small herds
through the well-maintained grounds,

                                  look at them.

Or rather, listen to them:

they low a diffuse science,
they eat leaves of Pliny
and lettuce,
they devour hamburgers,
Greek texts,
diminutive texticules in Sanskrit,

                              and then

they fertilize the earth
with classic detritus:

                alma mater.

If they belch,
an erudite dictum
perfumes the campus with sapience.

If, silent, they meditate,
swift, undecipherable syllogisms,
illuminating a pure universe,
cruise their fatigued neurons.
They search
—their gaze lost in the future—
for answers to the eternal
enigmas:

What will my salary be next year?
Is today Thursday?
                How long
will it take to melt so much snow?

ASÍ PARECE

Acusado por los críticos literarios de realista,
mis parientes en cambio me atribuyen
el defecto contrario;

                      afirman que no tengo
sentido alguno de la realidad.
Soy para ellos, sin duda, un funesto espectáculo:
analistas de textos, parientes de provincias,
he defraudado a todos, por lo visto;
¡qué le vamos a hacer!

Citaré algunos casos:

Ciertas tías devotas no pueden contenerse,
y lloran al mirarme.
Otras mucho más tímidas me hacen arroz con leche,
como cuando era niño,
y sonríen contritas, y me dicen:

                             qué alto,
si te viese tu padre . . . ,
y se quedan suspensas, sin saber qué añadir.

Sin embargo, no ignoro
que sus ambiguos gestos
disimulan
una sincera compasión irremediable
que brilla húmedamente en sus miradas
y en sus piadosos dientes postizos de conejo.

Y no sólo son ellas.

En las noches,
mi anciana tía Clotilde regresa de la tumba
para agitar ante mi rostro sus manos sarmentosas

SO IT SEEMS

Accused by literary critics of being a realist,
my relatives, on the other hand, say
the opposite about me:
                              they claim I have
no sense of reality.
For them I am, without a doubt, a sorry sight:
textual analysts, provincial relatives,
I have disappointed them all, it seems;
so what can I do!

I will cite some examples:

Certain devout aunts cannot contain themselves,
and they cry when they look at me.
Others are much more timid and make me rice pudding
like when I was a child,
and they smile contritely and say to me:
                                        how tall
you are, if your father could see you . . . ,
and they stop, not knowing what else to say.

However, I'm fully aware
that their ambiguous gestures
dissemble
a sincere, irremediable compassion
that shines wetly in their gazes
and in their pious, false rabbit-teeth.

And they're not the only ones.

At night,
my ancient aunt Clotilde returns from her tomb
to shake her scrawny hands in my face,

y repetir con tono admonitorio:
¡Con la belleza no se come! ¿Qué piensas que es la vida?

Por su parte,
mi madre ya difunta, con voz delgada y triste,
augura un lamentable final de mi existencia:
manicomios, asilos, calvicie, blenorragia.

Yo no sé qué decirles, y ellas
vuelven a su silencio.
Lo mismo, igual que entonces.
Como cuando era niño.
                    Parece
que no ha pasado la muerte por nosotros.

repeating in an admonitory tone:
You can't eat beauty! What do you think life is?

For her part,
my dead mother, in a thin, sad voice,
predicts a lamentable end to my life:
madhouses, nursing homes, baldness, gonorrhea.

I don't know what to tell them, and they
return to their silence.
It's the same, just as before.
Like when I was a child.
                       It seems
death has not passed between us.

EN SERIO

¿Qué te dimos en vida?

Te llamábamos
a veces por tu nombre
para decirte lo que nos dolía,
para pedirte cosas,

                para quejarnos
del frío
—como si fueses responsable del invierno—
o para preguntarte, suspicaces,
en dónde habías guardado esto o lo otro.

Pero
¿qué te dimos realmente?
¿Qué hubiéramos podido haberte dado
a ti, que no pedías,
que parecías no necesitar nada
más que estuviéramos allí, llamándote
a veces por tu nombre,
para pedirte siempre:
                  —danos, danos?

Acaso amor,
esa palabra impronunciable, impura.

Porque lo extraño es que tal vez te amábamos.
Pienso que te amábamos.
¡Ah, sí, cómo te amábamos!

Presenciamos inmóviles tu vida
y ahora, frente a tu muerte,
se nos vienen de pronto todas esas palabras
que no escucharás nunca.

SERIOUSLY

What did we give you when you were alive?

At times
we called you by your name
to tell you our pains,
to ask for something,
                    to complain
about the cold weather
—as if you were responsible for winter—
or to ask you, suspiciously,
where did you keep this or that.

But
what did we really give you?
What could we have given to you
if you, asking for nothing,
looked as if you needed nothing,
except that we be there, calling you
at times by your name,
always to ask for something:
                    —give us, give us?

Perhaps love,
that unpronouncable, impure word.

Because the strange thing is that perhaps we loved you.
I think we loved you.
Yes, how much we loved you!

Still, we contemplate your life
and now, faced with your death,
all these words you'll never hear
suddenly come to us.

ÁNGEL GONZÁLEZ: A CHRONOLOGY

1925   Born in Oviedo, Spain, the last of four children, just before the death of his father, a professor of pedagogy.

1934   Social Revolution of October is defeated and later repressed.

1936   Spanish civil war begins. Oviedo is left to the Francoists and besieged by the Republicans who are unable to liberate the city. His brother Manuel is assassinated; another brother, Pedro, goes into exile. His sister Maruja is prevented from working as a teacher. She is eventually allowed to teach in the public schools of Paramo del Sil.

1939   Spanish civil war ends; defeat of the Spanish Republic by Francoist forces.

1943   Stricken by tuberculosis and sent to Paramo del Sil. Begins to write poetry; studies poetry of Juan Ramón Jiménez and poets of the Group of 1927. Studies at the law school of the University of Oviedo. Lives in Paramo for three years and eventually takes the bar exam in Oviedo.

1950   Studies journalism in Madrid.

1954   Takes the examination for Civil Administration specialist. Enters the technical corps of the Civil Administration. Assigned to Sevilla.

1955   Promotion takes him to Barcelona for a year as proofreader for a variety of government publications. Becomes friends with Carlos Barral, Jaime Gil de Biedma, and Jose Augustin Goytisolo.

1956   *Áspero mundo* is published in Madrid. Runner-up for the important Adonais Prize for poetry. Returns to the Civil Administration in publishing in Madrid. Becomes friends with Gabriel Celaya, Juan Garcia Hortelano, Jose Amillo, Caballero Bonald, and other poets of his generation.

1961   *Sin esperanza con convencimiento* is published in Barcelona.

1962   *Grado elemental* is published in Paris; wins Antonio Machado Prize for poetry. *Grado elemental* contains poems of critical and social consciousness.

1965   *Palabra sobre palabra*, an edition of selected "poems for everyone," is published. Begins a brief series of love poems. Travels to England, France, Italy, and other European countries at the invitation of the Congress and Union of Writers.

1967   *Tratado de urbanismo* is published in Barcelona.

1968   La Editorial Seix Barral publishes his collected poems as *Palabra sobre palabra;* three more editions will follow.

1969   *Breves actaciones para una biografia* is published in Las Palmas de Gra Canaria. Death in Oviedo of his mother, María Muñiz.

1970   Travels to Mexico at the invitation of his friend Paco Ignacio Taibo. Befriends Luis Ríus.

1971   Returns to Spain and is invited to participate in a symposium on the Generation of 1956-1971 at the University of New Mexico, which also includes Jose Hierro, Blas de Otero, J. A. Valente, and Jaime Gil de Biedma.

1972   Becomes visiting professor during the spring semester at the University of New Mexico. *Procedimientos narrativos* is published in Santander. Second edition of *Palabra sobre palabra.*

1973   Returns to the United States as a visiting professor at the universities of Maryland, Texas, and Utah.

1974   Returns to the University of New Mexico as a professor of contemporary Spanish literature and makes Albuquerque his permanent residence.

1976   Publishes *Muestra . . .* in Madrid. Second edition of *Tratado de urbanismo.*

1977   Second corrected and augmented edition of *Muestra . . .* Third edition of *Palabra sobre palabra.* Miguel González Gerth publishes thirteen translations of González' in *The Texas Quarterly.* Publication of *Harsh World And Other Poems* by Princeton University Press in a translation by Donald Walsh.

1979   Travels to Cuba to serve as a juror for the Premio Casa de las Americas Poesia.

1983   *Prosmas o menos* is published.

1985   An augmented edition of *Prosmas o menos* is published. A second edition is published the same year. Receives the Premio Principe de Asturias de Las

Letras. Third edition of *Tratado de urbanismo*. Publication of "Guia para encuentro con Ángel González" for the collection *Luna de abajo* (Langreo, Asturias). This initiates a series of texts in Spain on González by poets, writers, and friends. An anthology with extensive bibliography is published.

1986   Fourth edition of *Palabra sobre palabra*, which includes new poems. Steven Ford Brown and Gutierrez Revuelta at University of Houston, Houston, Texas, begin collaborative translation project of González's collected poems.

1989   Publication of chapbook of English translations by Brown and Revuelta as *Word Upon Word,* published at the time of a reading and lecture by Ángel González, sponsored by the University of Houston, Rice University, and the Spanish Consulate. The *Mid-American Review* at Bowling Green University publishes a special feature of translations of González by Brown and Revuelta. Awarded the Angel Maria de Lera Hispanism Prize from the University of Colorado for his contributions to Hispanic culture. *Ángel González,* a critical anthology by Andrew Debicki, is published in Spain by Ediciones Jucar.

1991   González travels to West Germany and Italy. Receives the Salerno International Poetry Prize in Salerno, Italy. *Paintbrush,* a journal of poetry and translations at Northwest Missouri State University, publishes eight translations, an essay, and an interview with González by Brown and Revuelta.

1992   *En homenaje a Ángel González: ensayos, entrevista y poemas,* a collection of essays on the poetry of González, edited by Andrew Debicki and Sharon Keefe Ugalde, is published by the Society of Spanish and Spanish-American Studies at the University of Colorado.

1993   *Astonishing World: The Selected Poems of Ángel González, 1956-1986,* translated by Brown and Revuelta, edited by Brown, is published by Milkweed Editions.

Spanish chronology by
Paca Ignacio Taibo I.
Translated, with annotations,
by Steven Ford Brown.

TRANSLATORS' CREDITS

Aspero mundo: All translations are by Steven Ford Brown, except "Before I Could Call Myself Ángel González," "Death In The Evening," and "Human Geography" (with Gutierrez Revuelta); "To Some Poets" (with Moira Perez).

Sin esperanza con convencimiento: All translations are by Steven Ford Brown, except for "The Battlefield" (with Gutierrez Revuelta), "Of Two Words Now Made Clear" (with Cola Franzen), and "The Future" (with Moira Perez).

Grado elemental: All translations are by Steven Ford Brown, except "The Lessons Of Things" (primary translation by Moira Perez) and "Cemetery In Colliure" (with Moira Perez); and "The Lesson Of Literture" (with Cola Franzen); "This Moment" and "Elected By Acclamation" (with Gutierrez Revuelta).

Palabra sobre palabra: All translations are by Steven Ford Brown, except "The Word" (with Gutierrez Revuelta).

Tratado de urbanismo: All translations are by Steven Ford Brown, except "Public Park With Particular Legs," "The Mall," "Plaza With Towers And Palaces," and "Second Evocation" (with Gutierrez Revuelta); "Park For The Dead" (with Moira Perez); "Opulent Civilization" (with Cola Franzen).

Breves acotaciones: All translations are by Steven Ford Brown, except "Sometimes" and "I Snack On Some Afternoons" (with Gutierrez Revuelta); "My Profound Vocation" (with Moira Perez).

Procedimientos narrativos: All translations are by Steven Ford Brown, except "Of The Field Or Sea" (with Cola Franzen).

Muestra . . . : All translations are by Steven Ford Brown and Gutierrez Revuelta, except "Sometimes, In October, That's What Happens," "Horoscope For A Forgotten Dictator," "Again," and "Acoma, New Mexico" (by Steven Ford Brown); "Ode To The New Bards" (Steven Ford Brown and Moira Perez).

Prosemas o menos: All translations are by Steven Ford Brown and Gutierrez Revuelta, except "The Scandalous Rose," "The Christ Of Velazquez," and "Seriously" (by Steven Ford Brown).

Steven Ford Brown lives in Boston, where he edits The American Poets Profile Series and Ford-Brown & Co., Publishers. His criticism, interviews, poetry, and translations have appeared in *The Christian Science Monitor, Harvard Review, The International Quarterly, The Literary Review, Quarterly West, Rolling Stone, The Seneca Review,* and *The Texas Review.* A selection of prose poems from his book *The Sky Is Guilty Of An Oblique Considered Music* (Harrington-Black, 1991) was translated into Spanish and published in Argentina by Ofelia Castillo. Brown is the translator of *Exile: Twenty Poems Of Alejandra Pizarnik* (Harrington-Black, 1994), and is completing his translation of *I Never Asked To Be Born A Woman: The Selected Poems of Ana Maria Fagundo, 1965-1990.* He received a grant from the Ministerio de Cultura of Madrid, Spain, to assist in completing the translation of *Astonishing World.* He has given many readings of his poetry and translations on college and university campuses in the United States and Canada. He is currently making documentary films.

Gutierrez Revuelta was born in Madrid, Spain. He is the recipient of degrees from the University of Madrid and the University of California, San Diego. Since 1984 he has taught at the University of Houston, where he is presently an associate professor of Spanish. He has published four books of poetry : *We* (University of California, Irvine, 1981), *Present Love* (Atticus Press, 1982), *Complex Perspectives* (Editorial Origenes, 1988), and *Accidents and Other Resources* (Poesía Libertarias, 1990). In 1990 he received a National Endowment for the Arts fellowship for poetry. Funded by the Texas Commission on the Arts, Revuelta wrote and directed his play "The Blue Eustachian Tube (A Lorquian Farce in 1992 Scenes)," which had its premiere in Houston in 1992. He has written extensively on the poetry of Pablo Neruda and translated into Spanish the poetry of the Russian poet Andre de Korvin.

Designed by R. W. Scholes.
Titling in Bembo 14/16
and text in Bembo 12/14,
typeset by Susan Lynn Baldwin,
of Johnson Printing & Packaging Corp.
Printed on acid-free Odyssey Antique
by Princeton University Press.

More Translations from Milkweed Editions:

Amen
Poems by Yehuda Amichai
Translated from the Hebrew
by the author and Ted Hughes

The Art of Writing
Lu Chi's Wen Fu
Translated from the Chinese
by Sam Hamill

Circe's Mountain
Stories by Marie Luise Kaschnitz
Translated from the German
by Lisel Mueller

Clay and Star
Contemporary Bulgarian Poets
Translated and Edited
by Lisa Sapinkopf and Georgi Belev

The House in the Sand
Prose Poems by Pablo Neruda
Translated from the Spanish
by Dennis Maloney and Clark Zlotchew

Mouth to Mouth
Twelve Mexican Women Poets
Edited by Forrest Gander

Trusting Your Life To Water and Eternity
Twenty Poems by Olav H. Hauge
Translated from the Norwegian
by Robert Bly

8887